GENERATION NEXT

WHAT YOU NEED
TO KNOW ABOUT
TODAY'S YOUTH

GEORGE BARNA

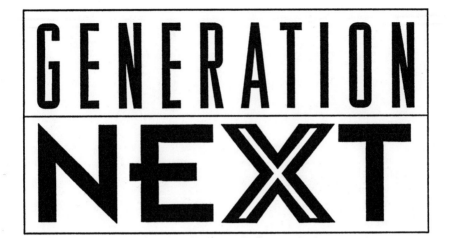

GENERATION NEXT

WHAT YOU NEED

TO KNOW ABOUT

TODAY'S YOUTH

GEORGE BARNA

AUTHOR OF *USER FRIENDLY CHURCHES* AND *THE FROG IN THE KETTLE*

Regal Books
A Division of Gospel Light
Ventura, California, U.S.A.

Regal Books
A Division of Gospel Light
Ventura, California, U.S.A.
Printed in U.S.A.

Regal Books is a ministry of Gospel Light, an evangelical Christian publisher dedicated to serving the local church. We believe God's vision for Gospel Light is to provide church leaders with biblical, user-friendly materials that will help them evangelize, disciple and minister to children, youth and families.

It is our prayer that this Regal book will help you discover biblical truth for your own life and help you meet the needs of others. May God richly bless you.

For a free catalog of resources from Regal Books/Gospel Light please contact your Christian supplier or call 1-800-4-GOSPEL.

Library of Congress Cataloging-in-Publication Data
Barna, George.
     Generation next / George Barna.
        p. cm.
     ISBN 0-8307-1809-5 (trade)
     1. Church work with teenagers. 2. Teenagers—United States—Religious life. 3. Evangelicalism—United States. I. Title.
BV4447.B36 1995   95-34581
259'.23—dc20   CIP

        4   5   6   7   8   9   10   11   12   13   14   /   02   01   00   99   98

Rights for publishing this book in other languages are contracted by Gospel Literature International (GLINT). GLINT also provides technical help for the adaptation, translation and publishing of Bible study resources and books in scores of languages worldwide. For further information, contact GLINT, P.O. Box 4060, Ontario, CA 91761-1003, U.S.A., or the publisher.

CONTENTS

942169

ACKNOWLEDGMENTS

Thank you to my family, friends, professional and ministry colleagues, and to the teenagers who helped this resource come into being.

Special thanks go to my friends at Regal Books, who flexed on the delivery deadlines so much that perhaps they should be renamed Gumby Productions. Bill Greig III and Kyle Duncan were their usual gracious selves in pretending that my wanton disregard for the calendar did not faze them. You'll know these guys by the number of jewels in their crowns.

My thanks, too, go to the staff at Barna Research, who handled the day-to-day affairs of the company while I was absent to write this book. Light up the applause sign for Nancy Barna, Gwen Ingram, George Maupin, Pam Tucker and Kelli Urban.

The most significant words of thanks go to my family for allowing me to abandon them for several days to focus on this project. My wife, Nancy, has been incredibly understanding and supportive during a very stressful period in which this book was written. The ministry and activities I engage in would not be possible if Nancy did not share the vision for ministry that drives me. She has been a champion of that vision and a strong helper in getting the job done, arduous piece by arduous piece. My daughters, Samantha and Corban, were also very generous in sparing Daddy. I pray that the impact of the book on how we touch the lives of young people will more than repay the sacrifices they made for the birthing of it.

INTRODUCTION

Not long ago, I spent two years as a leader in a high school ministry at the church I was attending. What an eye-opening time it was, getting to know and to share life experiences with the leaders of tomorrow. At times, it was refreshing and helped me lose track of my years and gray hairs. At other times, it made me painfully aware of my age and probably spawned more gray hair. Occasionally, I felt that God was able to use me in discernible ways to influence the lives of these soon-to-be adults. More often, I felt like I was drowning in a sea of irrelevance and ignorance (mine, not theirs).

The good news is that I survived the experience. My tenure as a teen group leader convinced me that there is nothing like extensive involvement in youth ministry to motivate adults to give heartfelt thanks to God for allowing us to have survived the pain, the agony and the frustrations of our teenage years so that we could endure the mere tortures and headaches of adult life. How intriguing our relationships were; neither side envied the other's problems. I looked with horror upon the constant flow of crises and challenges faced by my young friends, and decided I would not want to relive my teen years in today's environment. It was tough enough in the '70s; the '90s are brutal in comparison. Meanwhile, the teens sighed in relief that they did not have to contend with the steady diet of adult pressures that define my waking hours. Indeed, both teens and adults have unique filters through which they see life.

My foray into working with kids also renewed my belief that ministry to young people is one of the foremost means of ministry impact. Adults are a tough nut to crack: their life views are formed, their relational network is pretty much in place and their religious beliefs are usually determined. Trying to influence adults with the gospel, or to motivate them to make the gospel they have allegedly accepted evident—or, at least, significant—in their lives is a difficult task, on a good day. You can devote enormous levels of resources to adult ministry and have awfully little to show for the investment.

But teenagers are a whole different saga. We're talking about malleable minds, soft hearts—individuals desperately seeking help and hope. For an evangelical, young people are the fields for the harvest. For a teacher, these are the minds that sift through the information and really work it over until they are prepared to pass judgment on its veracity and utility. And for a leader who wants to influence lives for the sake of Christ, teenagers are probably the premiere frontier to penetrate. As an evangelical with the gifts of teaching and leading, working with teenagers made perfect sense. After all, teenagers are the leaders of the future. They are the challenge of the present day. And they are actually a lot of fun to be with in the process of having a positive impact.

Most significantly, I was impressed by the spiritual hunger of the kids. They'd never admit it, of course, either because they are not overtly aware that their spiritual journey is anything out of the ordinary, or because they would use different terms to express their condition. But when it comes to heavy-duty discussions about truth, meaning, purpose, life and death, and God, they're frontline players. They want discussions—not lectures—about these matters because they realize these are issues that count in life. Teens may have different learning styles from people of my generation, but they learn and they enjoy the discovery process. And spirituality is one arena of discovery that they view as being integrally connected to their personal maturity and life success.

WHAT THIS BOOK IS ABOUT

This is a book about people who are 13 to 18 years of age. About 22 million of this age group live in America today. They are a living paradox. At the same time that they are an incredibly rich source of ideas, energy and hope, they are also one of the most challenged and at-risk populations in our nation. Teenagers are an amazingly complex and challenging slice of the population to comprehend and with whom to interact.

This book is written for the 36 million adults who encounter teenagers every day in something more than a cursory fashion. These people include the 19 million parents living with these young people; the million or so teachers and extracurricular instructors they regularly encounter; nearly half a million church-based youth workers; three million employers; and the estimated 16 million merchants and sales clerks, law enforcement officers and other professionals who interact with teenagers each day.

My prayer is that the information and ideas contained in these pages will help to shape the thoughts and behavior of those of us who live, either intentionally or unwittingly, as agents of influence in the lives of America's teens. Whether we acknowledge it or not, we leave a lasting impression on the minds and hearts of teenagers. They are not beyond influence. But making a difference in the life of a teenager is radically different from influencing a younger child or an adult peer. Taking the time to have a positive impact is more than just "worth the effort"; it is a vital responsibility of every adult and a contribution to the future of our own existence.

I pray that you will glean from this book valuable information, principles and truths about teenagers in America in the late '90s. If you think it's scary raising them, you should try being one of them. This book may give you some insight into what that's like.

SOURCE OF INFORMATION

Before we get into the meat of the discussion, I should identify the source of the information that serves as the basis for my arguments. I have worked with kids in a ministry setting, have hired literally hundreds of teenagers in our business and have read extensively about the lives of teens and how to minister to them. If memory serves me correctly, I was once a teenager, (too) many years ago. In spite of these experiences, this book is based upon primary research.

In December 1994 and January 1995, we conducted a nationwide telephone survey among a random sample of teenagers. In total, we interviewed 723 kids whose ages ranged from 13 to 18, and whose selection was totally random. We talked to representative groups of kids from each age group in the 13 to 18 age span; kids from lower, middle and upper-class households; teens who were Caucasian, African-American, Asian-American and Hispanic-American; and kids who were churched and unchurched, Christian and non-Christian. Statistically speaking, the data for the entire sample are described as accurate to within plus or minus four percentage points at the 95 percent confidence level, based on sampling error estimates.

This book is my effort to distill each of those 25-minute conversations into a coherent picture of a confusing reality. Surveys are never completely accurate, nor are they accurate for prolonged periods of time, because things change rapidly these days. Surveys, however, do provide a relatively objective measure of conditions at a single point in time. If I were to base this book on my past experiences, personal perceptions and gut instincts, the result would be a very subjective point of view. That's not bad: Most books about youth are based on subjective experiences and, yet, many of those books are enormously helpful. Each such volume, however, runs the risk of discussing conditions, situations and opportunities that are unique to the author or the author's circumstances. Instead, I have chosen to rely heavily upon survey data, hoping this reliance on a less personalized source of input would offer a more useful read of today's youth culture and provide a panoramic view of our young people and their world.

Although the story that lies within these pages is necessarily influenced by my subjective experiences and perceptions—no analysis is ever completely objective—it is my hope that it contains enough unbiased perspective to enable you to interpret the information through your own subjective filters and to use the information wisely within your own unique context for ministry. In essence, I have boiled down all the data to a particular spin on teen reality. How you apply the insights and principles on these pages is really a matter that only you can reasonably determine. All I can say is: Be creative, be diligent, be biblical and be careful!

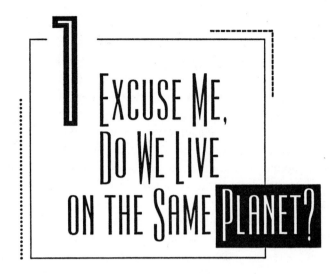

EXCUSE ME, DO WE LIVE ON THE SAME PLANET?

Bear with me for a minute as I relate two personal experiences that have jump-started my thinking about the state of youth today.

THAT WAS THEN...

It was probably in May of 1968. I was sitting on the sprawling front lawn of Princeton High School, just about to complete my freshman year in a competitive, upscale public high school in New Jersey. I was an oddity at the school, having a cadre of friends from each of the major social cliques: the jocks (athletes), greasers (car buffs), freaks (drug-crazed, antiestablishment hippies) and nerds (scholars). I had the marvelous advantage of knowing just about everything that was going on within the complex, subvisual, relational and behavioral terrain of the school. Even then, I liked having the pulse of the audience.

I had recently turned that broad base of relationships and insights into electoral victory: I had been voted class president, which for some reason seemed meaningful and important back then. But that day in May, as I sat on the lawn during a lunch break conversing with an eclectic group of friends, my mind turned to philosophical matters.

Jimi Hendrix's latest release was playing on my battery-driven portable tape recorder (it was, after all, a decade before the Walkman craze, and two decades before the first boom box hit the streets). A soft breeze was blowing the fragrance of freshly emerging honeysuckle across the landscape.

Most of us were stretched out on the lawn, propped up on our elbows, our legs pointing inward toward a common, if unconscious, midpoint, like the spokes of a wheel at rest. The spring sun felt good after a long winter; its warm rays brought a welcome tingle to my skin as I closed my eyes, listened to a few moments of Hendrix intoning the words to "All Along the Watchtower" and reflected.

For some reason long since forgotten, I was moved to share some innocent and naive pearls of wisdom with my comrades. "Ya know, life's okay. I think we're gonna make it once we get outta here and call our own shots. There's a lotta problems out there in the world, but we've got a chance to make a difference and to create something special in life. All this stuff here"—I paused, dramatically throwing my head in the direction of the school buildings a few hundred feet away—"all the classes and the grades and all, it's senseless—sheer nonsense. We're in a holding pattern, just marking time until we're ready to bring in a whole new way of thinking, a whole new set of values to live by. I can feel it. There's a new era coming, growing out of the new consciousness about war, the environment, public disgust with political corruption, openness to new kinds of relationships, even a de-emphasis upon money. Yeah, I gotta good feeling about the future."

Those were the philosophical musings of a 14-year-old on the brink of maturity. René Descartes I was not. And so we segued into a heated debate about who would win the American League pennant that year as the Grateful Dead followed Hendrix.

...THIS IS NOW

Jump ahead a quarter of a century to May 1992. I'm lying in a similar circle with four high-school guys I'm mentoring, an odd collection of lads who have latched on to me from our church's youth program. All of them attend one of the two high schools in Glendale, the upscale Los Angeles, California-area community where we live. Glendale may be well-to-do, but none of these young adults come from any semblance of affluence—all have a middle- or working-class background. But the diversity of my quartet transcends their demographics; their life views and behavioral patterns span the gamut.

Guy is eager to graduate so he can enter the military to get the discipline and guidance he desires in his life. His polar opposite within our foursome, Mark, is our resident restless spirit, quixotic and unreliable, lovable but frustrating. Unbeknownst to us at that moment, he will soon run away from his broken home in the vain hope of finding the total independence and freedom he desperately craves. Jeff and Alberto are followers rather than leaders; they are consistently drawn to the most convenient alternative that avails itself and seem to have no real plans or motivations beyond getting their next meal. Neither has much in the way of distinctives—both are average students, average athletes, average looking, average, average, average.

We're stretched out on the concrete walk outside the church's youth arena. Hendrix is absent from the boom box; this week Guns N' Roses is the heavy-metal band of choice. The spring breeze that blows through Glendale is neither new nor noteworthy, because Southern California only entertains two seasons—rainy and sunny, mostly sunny. In fact, few irregularities in our setting would distract my young friends from the focus of our time together: no girls to size up or impress, no authority figures to hide from or kiss up to, no pressing exams to study for, no part-time jobs to scurry off to and no group activities requiring our presence. When the initial banter is completed and a comfort level is established, I venture forth with a question that is, to me, significant and one that I hope will prove to be revealing. "So what do you make of life these days?"

To my relief, they take me seriously; there is no giggling or guffawing at the old dude asking the politically incorrect questions. But why would these guys laugh? Theirs is a generation that takes just about everything seriously. Theirs is a generation that constantly tackles such questions. No, they would take such a question at face value. And, after all, as the guitar player in the church's teen program, I've earned some degree of respect.

Mark, the impulsive, lead-with-your-heart-not-your-brains imp of the foursome, leads off. "Sometimes I wonder why we bother. Families don't work any longer. The schools are irrelevant to what we'll face in our careers. Friends, even my best friends, are so flaky and irresponsible that I can't count on them. Things cost too much, and I can't get enough cash to make it all happen. Girls have outrageous and unpredictable expectations. The environment is messed up, the political establishment is a failure. What's gonna bring it all back into focus, back into line?"

Jeff and Al vigorously nod their heads in agreement. This apparently serves as their contribution to the conversation.

Guy, less intelligent than Mark but eons more thoughtful, good-naturedly, but earnestly, challenges the remarks of his schoolmate. "But Mark, be realistic. You've got two options: Make it better or check out. You're probably not gonna give up, so what can you do about it? That's really the question for our generation. Yes, most families are dysfunctional, but why? What can we do to keep from raising dysfunctional families of our own? The economy is out of control and people's finances are a mess, but what can we do to restore some sanity to how we think about money and how we develop our views of greed and materialism? And think about your sex life, man, you of all people. Are you gonna continue to chase every babe that walks down the hallway, trying to score as if it were a baseball game? What about AIDS, Mark? What about STDs'? What about the implications of your treatment of that girl as a sex object?"

Guy was stuttering as he struggled to get the words out as fast as his brain and his heart pumped the thoughts to his mouth. He was on a philosophical roll now. "And what about balance in life? Is it gonna be working 14 hours a day and drinking beer till 2 in the morning, or will we try to have a richer life, one that allows for diversity and that provides some meaning? And violence? It's in our faces every day—you know that. They have armed guards at Hoover (High School). Jeannie was raped by some pervert last week. Billy G's dad was just carted off to jail for blowing away his boss in some fight they had at work. It's nuts out there—and it's all ours in a few years."

Guy paused as if he were the defense attorney about to levy the crushing summary statement. "No denyin' it, man, the people that came before us really screwed up the world, but it's gonna be up to us to clean it up and make it work again." He paused again, but this time he flashed an apologetic smile in my direction, realizing that his "people that came before us" reference was an allusion to my generation. "Well, you know..." he gamely explained before fixing his gaze back on Mark.

Jeff and Al again nodded their heads, with the same degree of intensity they had demonstrated after Mark's soliloquy. They feel strongly about Guy's dissenting view, too.

WHERE IS THIS CONVERSATION GOING?

The conversation went on for a good half hour, each fellow adding his thoughts, and often his fears, to the dialogue. At moments, I could relate to their sense of outrage at the state of the world they were going to inherit— a real mess. Sure, there are plenty of resources, but those were mostly beyond their reach, and there remains a sufficient quantity of good opportunities, but those, too, were generally outside of their control.

The thing that struck me most powerfully was the depth and sophistication of their grasp of the future. When I was growing up, back in the '60s and '70s, "quality of life" was not a concept my friends and I devoted much time to considering. Sure, we marched against the war, we railed against racism, we spawned the awareness of the generation gap and we welcomed the feminist mentality. But honestly, those thrusts were selfish. They were not about survival as much as they were meant to signal our arrival as a force too numerous and too energetic to be ignored. And for the vast majority of kids who were not political rebels and radicals, the existence, quality and nature of life was generally not a reality to be pondered and negotiated. The routine was simple: You got up in the morning, dealt with your parents as best you could, assessed the day's possibilities and connived your way into the best available situations, relationships and opportunities.

In contrast, my four junior colleagues of the '90s had an entirely different view of life and reality. Life, for today's teenagers, is serious stuff. They are not worried about who will be the homecoming king and queen, or what song is going to head Billboard's Top 40 next week. The magnitude of their anxieties are light-years beyond the comparatively lightweight matters that mesmerized my generation 20 or 30 years ago: whether to wear our hair long or short, how to get out of going to church next Sunday, or figuring out how to save up enough money to afford a nonchalant stroll to the Dairy Queen with the girl whose affections you were trying to win. The real visionaries of my class were scheming to save up enough money for a car or to have a college fund. But they were clearly in a class of their own.

Kids these days are arguing about the ethics of information privacy on the Internet (the telecommunications network that connects all on-line computer users, a veritable Infobahn of the age). They're engaging in verbal warfare about human dignity, personal responsibility and the lifestyle implications of globalism. They converse about quality of life as a matter of course. They know more about family structures and influence than we ever dared to contemplate. They may not be as well-schooled or even as articulate as our generation was, but today's youth are not idiots. They are more experienced, more thoughtful and less driven to conquer the world than we were at their age. That in itself speaks volumes about their intelligence and maturity.

Perhaps more than anything, I realized very quickly that my frame of reference for dealing with these kids was wholly inappropriate. I had jumped into teen ministry at my church thinking I would be working with kids who were just like I was 25 years ago, albeit a bit more high tech, more cynical, more worldly and dressed a bit grungier. Wake up, George! Realization number one: These are not kids. Perhaps the only thing youthful about them is their age.

The Six S's

This is, indeed, the *Reality Bites* generation (have you seen the movie?!). This is the group that has made Beavis and Butthead national icons. It's the group that supported, with high hopes, the presidential candidate who said he could feel their pain and who promised to respect and protect their future. Reality bites, indeed.

When asked to assess their own degree of satisfaction with life, teens are no different than adults. About 6 out of 10 say they are very satisfied with life, while the rest are less sanguine about their earthly experiences. What makes this especially intriguing is that, historically, teenagers have been more optimistic and enthusiastic about life than adults. After all, adults are saddled with numerous weighty, long-term realities: mortgages, taxes, child-raising issues, health problems, marriage stress and career challenges. Maybe it's just because I'm an adult now, but it seems only natural that adults would have a less sanguine view of the world. People who hold the responsibility always harbor a deeper level of concern and realism than those who are just along for the ride.

Of course, teenagers face obstructions, too, ranging from dating, sexuality and school to parents and money. But teens have typically emerged as sufficiently energized about their relative lack of heavy responsibilities and the plethora of unique and first-time opportunities that they have seen life as more fulfilling and exciting. But the times are changing.

You cannot conduct serious research among teenagers these days without concluding that, contrary to popular assumptions, there is substance to these young people. They clearly possess a core of insights and a commitment to world impact that often get overlooked by the media. They are more than just a generation of disillusioned whiners (although, superficially, a case can be made for such a characterization). They are more than simply a group of inadequately trained, underskilled, ambivalent worriers (although there is credible research to back this portrayal, too). A more comprehensive profile of these adults in youthful bodies shows that they have an intensity and a perspective about life that can be described by the following six "s" words.

They Are Serious About Life

Granted, today's teens love humor and reflect a sarcastic wit that betrays their fears, doubts and insecurities about life. But they are also savvy enough to know the score when it comes to the state of the economy, the environment, politics and government, morality, family, faith, racism and globalism. They are serious because they recognize that frivolity is for those who can afford such a devil-may-care attitude: they cannot. With quality of life issues at stake, they feel the weight of the bad decisions of past generations on their shoulders. Life is truly an unending series of trade-offs and compromises, fights and deals. Earlier than ever before, today's segment of teenagers realizes that their decisions today will shape significant aspects of their life from here on. And although it conflicts with the popular notion of modern teens, our research has discovered that teens believe that you reap what you sow. Consequently, they believe that they alone are responsible for what they ultimately get from life and they must, therefore, strive to make something worthwhile out of life.

They Are Stressed Out

Many sources of stress and anxiety are present in the typical teenager's life. School is a major stress. Family is another. Peer pressure is often overwhelming. Sexuality is baffling but ever-present. Techno-stress is very real, even to this generation that seems born to become software designers. Financial woes are widespread. The threat of crime is a daily challenge. Even the political correctness mind-set teenagers frequently embrace is a cause of stress. The current crop of teens is not the first to confront stress; it comes with the territory. Psychologists and sociologists, however, seem to concur that today's teens are drowning in a sea of tensions that threaten to paralyze them.

They Are Self-Reliant

Again, a hallmark of teenagers is their lust for freedom and independence. Teens in the mid-1990s, though, are raising the my-world-my-choice-my-turn style to a new art form. In some instances, this is out of necessity. One study we conducted showed that when it comes to homework and studying for tests—activities that are a central issue for millions of teens—parents fail to make the time, are unable to provide meaningful assistance or just cannot conquer the technology to render appropriate help. In other cases, teens are self-reliant because they believe they alone can make sense out of the issues: faith decisions are a prime example. Some of their self-reliance is a testimony to hormonal turbulence; some of it can be attributed to the predictable rebelliousness and arrogance of the age group. But a reason that is present to a larger degree than has historically been true is related to their understanding of how the world operates and their peculiar role within it.

They Are Skeptical

Whether this is a perspective mimicked from baby boomers or one learned through experience, most teenagers have little faith in the reliability of people, the assumed motivations behind people's actions, the viability of marketing claims, the ability of institutions to provide meaningful benefits, the existence of moral absolutes, the trustworthiness of journalists and the media, and the capacity of leaders to fulfill their promises. It is not so much that teenagers do not believe that good things can happen or that progress is unlikely; they simply reject prior claims regarding who will champion such gains, how they will be achieved, and what the benefits of alleged advances may be for themselves. Skepticism has become the psychological and emotional security system designed to shield them from disappointment.

They Are Highly Spiritual

Teenagers are not flocking to Christian churches, but they are intensely interested in spiritual matters. For some, this means following in their parents' footsteps and exploring the same religious route traveled by their parents. For an increasing number, however, their parents neither encourage a spiritual quest nor leave a spiritual legacy to explore. Thanks to ever-expanding access to information about different faith systems and a national obsession with diversity and tolerance, teenagers are investigating many divergent faiths. So far, they are either attaching themselves to an established religious group or following in the footsteps of many boomers by customizing a religious belief system that is personally appealing, if not internally consistent.

Many teenagers believe that a major component of America's illness is that we have lost our sense of the divine and the mystical. Millions of teenagers are seeking to incorporate their spiritual understanding into their daily existence, making faith more than a Sunday experience, but rather a life filter. Make no mistake about it though: "Spiritual" is no longer synonymous with "Christian."

They Are Survivors

Teenagers have an entirely different set of criteria for success and comparatively less passion for excellence and superiority than was true of boomers (and, to a lesser extent, the preboomer generation). Consequently, they may seem to be confused, complacent, less productive and to wrestle with a general unease about life. Let's realize, however, that these characterizations are coming through the analytical filter of societal leaders and cultural analysts—people whose view of teenagers is affected by standards of success and value grounded in the drive for excellence, an obsession with progress and the perception that bigger is better. From that perspective, it is reasonable to question whether or not teenagers will "make it" in life. They do not have the same passion for dominance. They are not as driven by an individualized lust for power, control and attention.

But teenagers will survive. They are not necessarily lethargic or lacking in motivation; it just seems that way to older people who operate on the basis of a different worldview and different personal goals. The truth is that teenagers are realistic, not idealistic. As such, they can handle a difficult cir- cumstance far better than many of their predecessors might have. Those predecessors, however, have little understanding of, or appreciation for, the manner in which teens assess, address and evaluate life situations and their responses to those conditions.

Note
1. STD is a commonly used abbreviation for a sexually transmitted disease, such as her- pes, gonorrhea or syphilis.

2 THE BIG PICTURE: CONCERNS AND CRISES OF YOUTH

As we shall see, many people overstate the anxieties and fears of youth, for various reasons. Yet it would be naive to overlook the concerns they themselves identify. How do they feel about their lives and what do they plan to do with them? What are their goals, the obstacles they suspect might challenge them, their dreams and hopes and fears?

LIFE-AND-DEATH DECISIONS

Given the lackadaisical attitude many teenagers demonstrate about life and personal development, it may shock you to find out that 7 out of 10 teenagers believe they have identified their purpose in life. Fewer *adults* claim they have actually identified their purpose or mission in life! But again, the differences are deceptive because they are based on a totally different framework of analysis and behavior.

Contrary to popular notions, few teens see their lives as being directionless or meaningless. It is adults, as outsiders looking in and assessing the perspectives and goals of young adults, who describe teenagers as lacking meaning and substance, based on the criteria for meaning and substance embraced by the adult generations. It seems that adults agonize about the direction of teenagers much more than teens worry about their own destiny.

Suicide may serve as a useful example of the gap in perspectives between the young and the old. Thirty years ago, when society's current leaders were teenagers, it was assumed that everyone wanted to live as long and as successfully as possible. Suicide was an unacceptable alternative, widely characterized as an escape route for the weak or a charitable solution for the deeply disturbed. Since that time, the suicide rate has climbed significantly.

The suicide rates released by the National Center for Health Statistics are generally provided for people in age groups defined as 5 to 14 and 15 to 24. The suicide rates for those in the 5 to 14 age bracket have more than tripled since 1950, rising from 0.2 per 100,000 population to 0.7. Among the 15- to 24-year-olds, the rate has also increased nearly threefold, jumping from 4.5 to 13.1 per 100,000 population. (See *The Universal Almanac 1995*, edited by John Wright, Andrews and McMeel, Kansas City, Kans., 1994, page 221.) In fact, based on further analysis of the data by others, we know that during the past decade or so the rate has risen considerably among 15- to 19-year-olds: from 8.5 per 100,000 population in 1980 to 11.0 in 1991. (These figures are from the National Center for Health Statistics data reported in the *Statistical Abstract of the United States - 1994*, U.S. Bureau of the Census, Washington, D.C., 1994.)

Now, suicide is viewed as just one of the many viable choices available to a healthy, functional young person. Many kids view it not as a sign of weakness, but as a rational choice in which the alternatives are less attractive. Today, the decision to reject suicide is a conscious statement of priorities and values. In essence, this is the first generation of teenagers who are intentionally making a choice between life (a decision that was initially made for them) and death (a decision that they may now control).

The live-or-die decision is not the only clear example of the difference in worldviews and perceived issues that separate teenagers from adults. The entire issue of purpose in life is another example of the age gap, especially between baby boomers (the parents of teenagers) and the teens. Baby boomers live to pursue their dreams, achieved through goal-setting and an aggressive determination to ascend the social, corporate and spiritual ladders by making their dreams become a reality.

Teenagers these days live to survive and see what happens. They would no sooner plan long-term strategies to bring their dreams to fruition than they would opt to outlaw baggy clothing. Baby boomers have been intent upon reshaping the world in their image, and creating an existence that undeniably bears their reflections. Teenagers are more comfortable implementing damage control procedures than they are championing a power-driven, bigger-is-better, unlimited growth future. In the end, boomers live for themselves. Teenagers live for themselves, too, but with a greater degree of sensitivity to the consequences of their choices upon the lives and choices of others.

THE CRISES OF YOUTH

You can tell a lot about a group by the issues it identifies as the most pressing or those that cause the greatest level of concern. Our research underscores the immediacy of life for teenagers. Their major anxieties and fears revolve around the short-term realities they face. Dreaming about the new millennium, an emerging new world order and other global innovations is foreign to the teen worldview. Their worldview is tangible and pragmatic. Having little stake in the power game of world politics and economics, the long-term positioning and personal power games that occupy the minds of their elders are totally irrelevant to them.

By far the most pressing concern troubling teenagers these days relates to their educational circumstances. This will surprise many people because we're used to reading reports stating that teenagers are primarily concerned about AIDS, the environment, racism, drug use and alcoholism. We know from our studies among teens that this list of concerns is of significance to those who are 13 to 18 years of age; however, we know just as certainly that these are not the worries that fill their daydreams, their nightmares and their philosophical deliberations.

This makes sense, given the practical bent of American teens. AIDS, for instance, is a dreaded disease and one that is a growing threat to young lives. But few teens have ever met anyone who has died from AIDS. It is not sufficiently real to them for it to be a life-changing concern at the moment. In our national survey of teenagers, when asked to list the top two or three most pressing issues they are facing, AIDS was named by only 1 percent of the group! Yet AIDS exists as an ever-present irritant residing in the recesses of their minds, an issue to be acknowledged and recognized, but not necessarily one that drives their moment-to-moment decision making.

Environmental decay is a politically sexy issue that can get teenagers excited. But our research shows that their excitement about environmental protection wanes quickly. The typical baby buster who gets involved in an environmental cause lasts an average of less than one year in service to the cause; his investment is intense but short lived. More importantly, environmentalism is a trump card they can pull out in debates with the adults whose generation has mismanaged the environment. Sure, they care about creating a sustainable lifestyle and a clean planet; but again, this is not one of the driving forces in their ongoing decision making. In some ways, it is worse: like AIDS, it lurks in their minds as a looming disaster about which they may have no control or contribution.

Drug abuse is a perpetual and hot political topic because it has the ability to fan the flames of emotion and is a politically safe cause to champion: nobody wants to support drug abuse. The government's statistics show, however, that drug abuse affects a very small proportion of people. More importantly, drug abuse has declined precipitously among young people in the past two decades. Most of the kids have either tried drugs or know peers who have. Drugs are a commodity that both fascinates and scares most kids. But relatively few of them, despite their awareness of the devastating effect of drug abuse on the lives of thousands of teens, are either haunted or shaped by the specter of drug abuse. Whether it is because of ego ("It can't hurt me"), ignorance ("Me and my friends aren't into that stuff") or overkill ("It's just a big media hype"), drug abuse is not among the gravest personal concerns of teenagers.

The issue that troubles kids the most is their educational performance. School-related woes outnumber any other concern by more than a three to one margin; almost half of all teenagers (45 percent) said at least one of their top-ranked personal concerns was related to education. The primary dilemmas related to education are getting the grades they want, getting into the college they desire and being able to complete their homework consistently.

Why is schooling such a crisis? Think about their world. Parents show more interest in the school achievement of their kids than in almost any other aspect of teen life, including their character development. People often judge the intelligence and future potential of young people by their classroom record. Even peer relationships are influenced by academic status. A large share of teenagers' waking hours is consumed by educational activities. The kinds of lifestyle issues that do concern them—from sexual involvement and friendships to jobs, finances and physical safety—are all affected by what takes place at school or in relation to their education. They know that the people who get ahead are most frequently those who use education to their advantage.

What else troubles today's teenagers? The next most pressing items are difficulties with personal relationships (mostly in relation to peers, less frequently in relation to parents); handling pressure (primarily peer pressure, pressure to have sex or to take drugs, drinks or cigarettes); the threat of physical danger or crime; and financial needs or challenges.

Notice that the dominant crises are immediate and short term. That's the way teenagers think and live, more than ever before. They are not overly concerned about things that may be significant problems eons from now—such as health and career decisions and opportunities. Also, recognize that teenagers do not tend to think about underlying causes as much as they wish to confront the outgrowths of those causes. For example, morality and values are a frontline issue for just 1 out of every 20 kids. Faith decisions and choices are of pressing concern to 1 out of every 25 teens.

TEEN DREAMS

When pressed to think about the future, teenagers reveal that they want much the same thing most Americans desire these days: happiness, inner peace, comfort and so on. In more practical terms, though, that means that

---

TABLE 2.1

WHAT ARE THE MAJOR ISSUES CONCERNING TEENAGERS?

Education-related concerns 45%
Relationships 24
Emotional pressure 17
Physical threats, violence 13
Financial difficulties 13
Substance abuse 11
Morality and values 5
Career considerations 5
Health issues 4
Religious issues or decisions 4

---

teens want good physical health, close personal friends whom they can count on, a comfortable lifestyle and a single marriage partner who will be with them for life. These elements are deemed highly desirable by at least four out of every five teenagers.

Somewhat less significant, but still considered highly desirable by at least 6 out of 10 teenagers, is having a clear purpose in life, having a spouse and children, living with a high degree of integrity and having a high-paying job. Between 50 and 58 percent of the teen population—a slim majority—indicate that they think having a close relationship with God, having a satisfying sex life with a marriage partner, making a difference in the world and influencing other people's lives would be very desirable.

The elements that are least compelling to contemporary teens include living close to family and relatives, owning a large home; being active in a local church and achieving fame or public recognition.

Categorically, our research suggests that teenagers are not nearly as driven as the boomers were to make a difference in the world. Their goals are not nearly as materialistic, nor as power driven. Overall, teens are attracted by

TABLE 2.2

LIFE CONDITIONS TEENAGERS CONSIDER TO BE VERY DESIRABLE

Having good physical health 90%
Having close personal friendships . . . . ' 84
Having a comfortable lifestyle 82
Having one marriage partner for life 80
Having a clear purpose for living 79
Having a spouse and children 69
Living with a high degree of integrity 61
Having a high-paying job 60
Having a close relationship with God 58
Having a satisfying sex life with a marriage partner 57
Influencing other people's lives 53
Making a difference in the world 53
Living close to family and relatives 44
Owning a large home 37
Being personally active in a local church 37
Achieving fame or recognition 21

the possibility of direction, emotional wholeness and the development of their own families.

Our research suggests that a change in desired life outcomes occurs between the ages of 13 and 14. During that time, which is a major transition point for many kids as they graduate from junior high to senior high, they begin to shed some of their materialistic urges (e.g., high-salaried occupation, large home) and their interest in religious activity (e.g., relationship with God, church involvement). Sexual relationships become a preoccupation around age 15 and 16. Personal integrity is not a strong issue until age 17.

Gender also influences the objectives of young people. Boys are much more interested in having a satisfying sex life and achieving fame. Girls are notably more desirous of having one marriage partner for life, living close to relatives, influencing other people's lives and making a difference in the world. Although it is dangerous to trumpet stereotypes, it appears the

TABLE **2.3**

What Teenagers Deem Very Desirable, by Age and Gender

Very Desirable Outcome	Age					Gender	
	13	14	15	16	17	Boys	Girls
Having good physical health	90%	90%	92%	91%	86%	87%	92%
Having close personal friendships	85	79	86	83	88	83	85
Having a comfortable lifestyle	86	78	85	85	78	83	82
Having one marriage partner for life	80	80	76	81	84	74	86
Having a clear purpose for living	79	69	81	79	81	77	80
Having a spouse and children	70	67	75	66	69	67	72
Living with a high degree of integrity	56	56	59	62	72	62	60
Having a high-paying job	68	56	58	59	58	61	59
Having a close relationship with God	66	59	56	55	52	55	60
Having a satisfying sex life with a marriage partner	47	47	56	66	64	64	50
Influencing other people's lives	58	47	55	51	55	49	57
Making a difference in the world	52	58	50	51	52	45	59
Living close to family and relatives	47	48	41	44	42	37	50
Owning a large home	44	30	37	40	32	40	35
Being personally active in a local church	42	35	35	38	34	35	39
Achieving fame or recognition	24	18	20	23	18	28	15

axiom that girls have more traditional, outer-oriented values while boys are more selfish and base in their desires has some basis in reality.

It is also apparent that the transition from junior high to senior high rad-

TABLE 2.4

A COMPARISON OF WHAT ADULTS AND TEENAGERS DEEM VERY DESIRABLE

Very Desirable Lifestyle	Teens	Adults
Having good physical health	90%	91%
Having close personal friendships	84	79
Having a comfortable lifestyle	82	72
Having a clear purpose for living	79	80
Having a high-paying job	60	43
Having a close relationship with God	58	74
Influencing other people's lives	53	39
Living close to family and relatives	44	63
Owning a large home	37	30
Being active in a local church	37	49
Achieving fame or recognition	21	10

ically shakes up the values and worldview of the typical youth, but that the pattern of values and interests is restored after a year or so (i.e., by age 15) to levels similar to those of 13-year-olds. This is interesting because it confirms the anecdotal evidence of counselors and psychologists who suggest that if children suffer from severe lack of direction or absence of goals and values by the time they reach their teen years, it is often too late to have any significant influence on their subsequent behavioral patterns. After studying patterns of faith for years, our research leads to a similar prognosis: if children are not reached with the gospel by age 13, the chances of their accepting the gospel after that point are greatly reduced.

LIKE PARENT, LIKE CHILD

We have also found that a lot of the views embraced by teens are a mirror image of those espoused by their parents. For instance, when it comes to matters of faith, adults are much more interested in having a close relationship with God or being an active participant in a local church. This is particularly striking because adults are much less likely to desire these characteristics than was true a decade or two in the past. This decline in interest in traditional religious endeavors, however, may have influenced young adults; perceiving the decreasing sense of significance of traditional spirituality, teenagers may be searching for lifestyle components that they see as more relevant and valued.

Teenagers differ from adults in other perspectives, too. They rate much higher on those elements that smack of materialism or affluence. They are more likely to desire a comfortable lifestyle, a high-paying job, owning a large home and achieving fame or public recognition. What makes this especially intriguing is that in conversation young people are frequently critical of the selfishness and acquisition-driven lifestyles of their elders. They express a desire to lead a simpler life and one that is more sympathetic to the environment and the needy. In comparison to older people, though, they emerge as a generation that is less up front about their desire to lead "the good life," but that has a clear zeal for such an existence.

Another distinction worth noting is that youths seem to be more driven to have an influence in the lives of other people. Almost two-thirds of the teenagers we interviewed said having interpersonal influence is very desirable, while less than half of the adults we interviewed concurred. The implications of this difference are interesting. Influence, of course, is the core of leadership, and one of the defining characteristics of the boomer generation is that it has thus far failed to produce strong leaders in the public arenas (i.e., politics, education, religion). We could be witnessing the seeds of leadership that need to be nurtured so that this next generation, as it moves into positions of decision making and authority, will have stronger leaders and, thereby, avoid many of the crises and paradoxes that plague the boomer and builder generations today.[1]

ON ABSOLUTE TRUTH

The desired future just described is a reflection of a new pool of attitudes and views that define the heart of teenagers. In some cases, we find that the perspectives are parallel to those held by adults at-large; in other instances, teenagers are pushing the envelope farther than adults have dared to (so far).

Consider the issue of truth. About three-quarters of all adults reject the notion that there are absolute moral truths. Most Americans believe that all truth is relative to the situation and the individuals involved. Similarly, at least three-quarters of our teens embrace the same position regarding moral

TABLE 2.5

TEEN ATTITUDES

Statement	Agree	Disagree	Don't Know
Related to truth:			
What is right for one person in a given situation might not be right for another person in a similar situation. 91%	8%	1%
When it comes to matters of morals and ethics, truth means different things to different people; no one can be absolutely positive that they know the truth. 80	19	1
There is no such thing as "absolute truth"; two people could define "truth" in conflicting ways and both be correct. 72	28	*
The Bible provides a clear and totally accurate description of moral truth. 72	27	2
Lying is sometimes necessary. 57	42	1
Related to faith:			
God established limits for humankind; acting in conflict with His laws has negative consequences. 61	35	4
The Bible does not provide practical standards for living in today's world. 27	71	3
Anyone who relies upon the Bible or religious faith for moral guidance is foolish . .10	90	0
Related to worldview and lifestyle:			
The main purpose of life is enjoyment and personal fulfillment. 64	36	*
You know that something is morally or ethically right if it works. 42	57	1
One person cannot really make much of a difference in this world. 17	83	*

(*indicates less than one-half of 1 percent gave this response.)

truths. Not only do more than three out of four teenagers say there is no absolute moral truth; four out of five also claim that nobody can know for certain whether or not they actually know what truth is. This may also help to explain why a majority of teenagers (57 percent) say that lying is sometimes necessary—not merely convenient, common, understandable or acceptable, but *necessary*.

But teens are caught in a paradox. At the same time as three out of four assert that the Bible provides a clear and totally accurate description of moral truth, a large majority of those same individuals argue that there is no such thing as absolute truth. This is clearly a self-contradictory perspective.

Why is there this seemingly glaring and obvious discrepancy? There seem to be four primary explanations. First, many teenagers use the words "moral" and "truth," but really do not know what they mean. Theirs is a vague understanding of truth and morality—"stuff that has to do with right and wrong." Thus, when they talk about "absolute" moral truth, they're not really sure what we're talking about, even when an explanation is provided. This speaks volumes to those of us who have become comfortable with such language that we use it in our teaching and conversation with teens. Unfortunately, teens probably don't have a clue what we're babbling on about!

Second, some teens are willing to state that the Bible contains absolute truth claims, but because they have not and do not read the Bible, those claims may as well not exist. For millions of teens, the issue is not that they are opposed to the Bible, but rather that the contents of the Bible are simply not a part of their experience. As a result, any insights or wisdom it contains are beyond their comprehension or concern.

For millions of others, the Bible is viewed as a decent book for some people, but one that teens perceive to be irrelevant to their own lives because it does not convey useful principles or standards. Because the Bible and most religious activities are foreign to them and seem irrelevant to what "real life" is all about, they perceive two parallel worlds coexisting: the spiritual, impractical world that contains many pure and absolute (and impractical) dictums (such as truth, morality, love, faith), and the real world, the one they inhabit, which deals with the hard stuff of daily living. Truth may be a wonderful concept, but many teens don't have sufficient interest in such an "impractical" or unrealistic concept to explore it further. Millions of those who do have the interest do not have the philosophical, intellectual, and spiritual foundations to take such an exploration to the next level.

Third, many kids seem to distinguish between the *concept* of truth and the *practice* of truth. Sure, they'll allow that there may be a definitive body of truth somewhere—perhaps in the Bible, perhaps elsewhere. But in their personal reality, truth is always relative to the individual and to the situation.

In fact, the intellectual and emotional separation many teens make between impersonal absolute truth and personal truth is very crucial to understanding them. Most teenagers believe that some truth may well be explicated in the Bible. They are perfectly willing to let people who dig for those nuggets of wisdom and insight live according to them. But they are not willing to suggest that the alleged truths in the Bible are the only truths, or the most important truths, or even that they are personally relevant truths. Thus, the truth that may be in the Bible is seen in relativistic terms: If the Bible contains your truth, so be it; allow everyone to find his or her own sources of truth and to deal with those perspectives accordingly.

Fourth, we have found that today's young people, probably more than recent generations of youth, are perfectly capable of living with intellectual contradictions. They are comfortable with the fact that some form of truth exists, but is not influencing their personal thoughts or behavior. Again, theirs is a tangible world; survival is more pertinent and real to them than intellectual consistency or perfect wisdom. If they possess inherently contradictory views, so be it. As long as they can get by from day to day, and have some degree of enjoyment and personal fulfillment, don't rock the boat. After all, if it ain't broke, don't fix it.

Matters of faith raise some similarly interesting insights. Again, part of the intrigue is recognizing that teenagers hold some views that stand in vivid contrast to their behavior. Their views about Christian faith are relatively on target. Three out of five assert that God has established limits for people, and that ignoring those limitations brings undesirable consequences. Three out of four contend that the Bible contains practical principles for living successfully these days. And only 1 out of every 10 teenagers believes that people who rely upon the Bible or their religious faith for guidance are acting foolishly. And yet, their perspectives and behavior are barely influenced by the Bible, faith or other religious experiences and perspectives.

In the end, teenagers, like their parents, possess a rather selfish, tangible, secularized view of life: We are on earth only to wring as much pleasure, fulfillment and joy out of the experience as possible. Much of teens' activity is measured in very momentary and tangible terms: If it works, it's right and good; if it fails, it's inappropriate and wrong. Remember, of course, that right and wrong are conditional. And in the process, if they are able to assist others in viewing the world as they do, they then have an opportunity to make a difference in the world. Teenagers may not be idealistic, but they do believe they can still redeem crucial components of our present-day existence in line with their personal perspectives of right and wrong, success and failure, significance and meaninglessness.

Note

1. Throughout this book, mention will be made of the nation's four adult generations. Teenagers are part of the baby buster generation, the group born between 1965 and 1983. The baby boomers, the nation's largest generation ever, are those born from 1946 to 1964. The preceding generation are the builders, the small but driven generation who bridged traditional values with a wartime "we can make America a world leader" mentality; they were born from 1926 through 1945. People born prior to 1926 will simply be referred to as seniors in this text. For a more complete description of the definitions and differences among these groups, see George Barna, *Baby Busters: The Disillusioned Generation* (Chicago: Northfield Publishing, 1994).

3
THE
CHARACTER OF
OUR TEENS

On a recent trip through Thailand, one of our guides explained to us how elephants are trained. When an elephant is very young, it is tied to an immovable stake, much in the same way as a horse may be tied to a hitching post. Unable to break free from the stake, the young elephant eventually stops trying to escape from the rope and stake that limit its range. The animal's owners then have greater freedom in the selection of supports on which to tie the elephant. Sometimes the owners may use just a small wooden stake that is tenuously implanted in the ground. Trained to believe the stake is not going to give, the elephant does not attempt to break loose.

As the elephant grows bigger and older it gains the strength to easily yank the stake out of the ground and gain access to a wider area. Because the bulky pachyderm was trained right from the start that its access is restricted to the area defined by the length of the rope around its neck, however, it does not try to expand its territorial horizons.

Teenagers might be thought of in a similar way—not the rope around the neck part, which many parents, teachers and youth leaders have considered, but the part about reacting to circumstances and opportunities in response to their conditioning and their resulting self-perceptions. As a generation that is more reflective than the action-oriented boomers who came before them, the perspectives of today's teenagers about their character and abilities are substantially different in comparison to the teenagers of the past several decades.

A SELF-PORTRAIT

When teenagers describe themselves, the profile that emerges is different from what is expected. Although their generation is, in general, less optimistic and excited about the future than were prior generations of young people, they nevertheless portray themselves in a positive light.

Given a list of adjectives to describe themselves, their choices are startling in comparison to the conventional wisdom about teens. Consider these outcomes drawn from a recent national survey we conducted among a representative sample of teenagers.[1]

- Four out of five describe themselves as "excited about life."
- Three out of four say they are "trusting of other people."
- Three out of four claim to be "optimistic about the future."
- Two out of three see themselves as "a leader."
- Two out of three believe they are "physically attractive."
- Just over half (56 percent) contend that they are "religious."
- Two out of every five admit to being "stressed out."
- Only one out of every eight suggest they are "lonely."
- A mere 12 percent use the term "discouraged" to describe themselves.

Does this sound like a profile of a group of losers and individuals who believe they possess little value, little hope and little joy? Hardly. From where, then, do we get all the media hype about a generation of disillusioned, sullen, hopeless, angry and depressed youth?

Let me suggest a few possibilities. The contrarian view of today's kids does not emanate from any single source. Put the following pieces together, however, and you'll find the puzzle that emerges is of a young adult population that may, in fact, be less mainstream than were past classes of teens.

Hyping Generation X

Teenagers are part of the baby bust generation, which the media have enjoyed lampooning as the hapless, hopeless "Generation X." To the disadvantage and chagrin of teens, the behavior and views of the entire buster generation, which is now dominated by people who are 19 to 30 years old, are assigned to teens. The truth of the matter is that teenagers are only a small part of that generation and they do not necessarily reflect the same thoughts and behaviors as the older busters—well, not yet anyway.

Pretransition Period

A transition period seems to take place between the ages of 18 and 25 during which many transformations occur in the worldview, relationships, values, beliefs and lifestyles of young people. During this period, they experience some of the freedoms they have desired for so long, and their idealism and hope fades.

Jobs are less fun and less lucrative than expected. Church attendance becomes a practice of the past, diminishing the significance of religion. Family becomes an emergency support system rather than a daily security blanket. Education becomes serious stuff, rather than merely a precursor to college realities. Sexual relationships become more laden with long-term implications and treacherous emotional minefields. The cost of living changes from a newspaper expression to a personal challenge. As yesterday's teens have shifted into the independent adult role, we have watched their attitudes and lifestyles take a turn to the pessimistic. That demise of hope is often assumed to characterize the views of teenagers as well.

Futility and Stress

In comparison to past teenage segments, the current group actually is less sanguine about life. We know, for instance, that feeling stressed out about life has increased from 25 percent in 1990 to nearly 40 percent today. Other changes in attitude and demeanor include a heightened sense of the futility of politics; a huge increase in the proportion who live with the fear of being the victim of a physical crime; a rise in the discouraging assumption that they will not be able to afford an education, a house and a comfortable lifestyle; and less belief in the ability of traditional social institutions, such as marriage and religion, to provide order and predictability to life. In fact, we also find that fewer kids now believe they will be able to fulfill their dreams or to achieve the ever-elusive goal of "happiness."[2]

Outside Interpretations

The behaviors and words of teens are interpreted by adults within the prevailing cultural context. Those interpretations by others, rather than the actual self-views of teens or their true motivations, often serve as the description of the teen population. Twenty years ago, when teenagers used profanity in public it was viewed as an attempt to rebel or to draw attention. Today, it is viewed as a natural part of society's cultural change. Back then, kids who went to the science club or computer lab were deemed eggheads; today, we assume that silicon runs in their veins. When a group of kids got together in the early '70s we assumed it was either to start a demonstration against the war or to initiate a sports competition. Today, we immediately worry about street gangs.

Two decades ago, kids went to church because their parents accompanied them. These days, fewer and fewer parents are attending; the kids are seeking spiritual direction through alternative means. Two decades ago, the drugs of choice were marijuana and hashish; now, it's alcohol. It used to be a big deal for teens to sneak into an R-rated movie. Currently, it's hard to find theaters that challenge the age of ticket buyers. Consequently, in this new cultural context, the same behavior carried out today may be interpreted entirely differently from what it was in the past—even though it may be driven by the same motivations as in the past.

Values in Motion

The values and leisure preferences of teens are changing all the time. This is at least partly attributable to new technologies and to significant changes in family structures and relationships. Yet, many social analysts continue to characterize teens in light of traditional expectations and lifestyles, rather than in the prevailing context. This results in teenagers being cast as valueless, lazy and unsupportive of family. In reality, they are not valueless, because the absence of values is impossible. Instead, teenagers today simply have more fluid, less influential, values. Their values seem unorthodox compared to those of the builder and senior generations, but they are values nevertheless.

Teenagers' apparent apathy may be chalked up to not having the same achievement-based goals as most adults have, and thus they are less motivated to produce. And they are not really unsupportive of family. On the contrary, they are scared of becoming too dependent upon their families because so many families wind up being divided, creating serious emotional damage to those who relied upon the family for stability and connectedness.

The Self-Perception Gap

Researchers are well aware that a person's self-image may have only a slim relationship to the image of that person held by the world at large. Think about it. How often have you met a person who thinks he or she is a brilliant conversationalist, but your assessment is that the person is a world-class bore? How many people do you know who believe they do wonderful work on the job, but who are merely average producers, at best? Have you ever attended a church where the pastor regularly gives sermons he believes are insightful and witty, but you characterize as part of God's punishment for your sins?

The same principle is at work in the self-perceptions of teenagers. Believe me, two-thirds of them are not leaders, no matter what they think of themselves. When you begin to press them for specifics about their fears, expectations and disappointments, more than one-eighth of them are discouraged about the future. Their trust of people may mean they are willing to listen to what others have to say, but consistently giving others the benefit of the doubt or believing that what they say is true is the exception to the rule. And although this is a relational group of people, millions of them have yet to figure out how to build lasting, substantive relationships with other people. Lonely? They'd hate to admit it because that's tantamount to saying they have failed in their efforts to be popular and connected. For some teens who place a premium upon connectedness, admission of such failure is too much.

But we ought not to castigate teenagers for their erroneous self-perceptions; it's a behavior that was modeled for them by their parents.

The self-portrait teenagers paint is not so much designed to mislead people as to anesthetize themselves to the harsh realities of today's life. Given our earlier discussion that their decisions not to commit suicide is a rational choice and a statement about life, it may be that by having crossed the "live or not to live" threshold they are now confronting some of the consequences of their choices. Having chosen to continue their lives, they must now figure out how to successfully handle the tensions and pressures of a world they do not control and which seems to be constantly flirting with disaster. Their indefensibly positive self-view is simply one way of handling all that the world is throwing their way.

Psychologists tell us happiness is a state of mind rather than a state of being. Teenagers may have unconsciously discovered and embraced this principle. If they believe they can cope, then they can cope. If they believe in themselves, then they have worth. If they contend that they can make the world a better place to live, then they are more likely to create that better place.

CRACKING UNDER PRESSURE

It is important to recognize the growing crisis of stress that is engulfing teenagers. We are approaching a time when half of all teenagers will suffer from an acute sense of pressure; half of the 17-year-olds in America already claim they are stressed out. The teen years have always been a tense phase of life, but the tension has traditionally come from sources such as surging hormones, college entrance exams and the growing sense of urgency to flex one's independence.

Angst Beyond Their Age

The tensions our kids wrestle with these days transcend the usual pressures of maturation. The new parcel of pressures are imposed by a less tolerant adult society upon an increasingly amenable youth population. Responsibilities that used to be reserved for young adults in their post-high school days are now routinely thrust upon the scrawny shoulders of 13- and 14-year-olds. And these pressures are not just intensive, but also extensive: to perform academically, to balance technology and feelings, to enjoy leisure opportunities, to make wise financial decisions, to deal with sexual tensions intelligently, to balance family and personal needs, to be a good citizen in an age of hyperindependence, to remain connected to the group without abandoning individuality, to get involved in causes that count, to find meaning in life and to watch out for one's personal security (e.g., reputation, crime, violence).

As adults, we look at this laundry list of angst-producing responsibilities and shrug our shoulders: This is just part of the daily regimen for us. But the difference is that teenagers are, well, teenagers; they're just kids. They have not had the requisite time to explore the mysteries and snares of the world without external expectations. They have not had the opportunity to plumb the depths of their characters, to figure out who they really are or to learn more about what is really important to them. They have been robbed of the incubation period necessary to allow their minds, bodies and spirits to develop more fully and get in synch before dealing with the enormously complex realities of life in a "civilized" society at the close of the twentieth century.

High Expectations

Why the rush to turn teenagers into fully (dys)functional adults? One key is to realize that expectations in America have become out of control. People expect outrageous things of us and we, in turn, put pressure on those around us to perform beyond their capabilities. Consider some of the situations in which we place our kids.

We expect them to develop a viable values system, even though schools are warned to avoid the communication of values, churches have failed to teach a practical and coherent set of values, and parents continue to abdicate the responsibility for passing on a values system to their offspring. No wonder teenagers are baffled about values: Few adults understand the debate, although they intuitively know that values are important!

We demand that teenagers play by adult rules and standards, even though the youngsters are not adequately prepared to compete in the adult world. So, for instance, we send competing and conflicting messages about sexuality, then gasp in horror when teens announce their involvement in a pregnancy. We encourage them to grow in their knowledge and appreciation of technology; then rail about how much time they spend with cable TV, videos, Nintendo and America On-Line. We invite them to embrace role models, but shudder when they list Howard Stern, Eddie Vedder, Madonna, Johnny Depp, Courtney Love and Bart Simpson as the people they would most like to emulate.

In short, what we have done is to remove the wall of defense between our children and the world of adult responsibilities. Where parents used to guard their kids from being overwhelmed, many no longer protect them.

TABLE 3.1		
"A" Students	Self-Description of Teens	"C" Students
88%	Excited about life	74%
85	Trusting of people	77
83	Optimistic about the future	58
72	A leader	53
66	Religious	43
34	Stressed out	48
9	Lonely	18
8	Discouraged	18

And adult tolerance for teen growth has also waned. Adults are used to confusing doing our best with producing the best we can, and we now place the same burdens on our kids. In demanding the unachievable of teens, we blur the distinction between excellence and perfection.

Stress will increasingly emerge as a major factor in the lives of our teens. Many of us may not recognize its effects until they are evident in the perspectives and behaviors of these youngsters as young adults in the marketplace. You will probably experience the outgrowth of their sense of stress even now in the lethargic attitude they demonstrate toward taking on new tasks, meeting achievement goals and deadlines, and seeking closure on tasks as diverse as college (the four-year program is unappealing and uncommon these days), completing books they begin reading and thinking through their purpose in life.

Relief from the Tension

Our research also highlighted the fact that kids who do well in school and those who believe they have identified their purpose in life (for the moment, at least) are more likely than their peers to feel good about themselves and their future. What we don't know is which causes the other: does achievement create a positive view of the future, or does an upbeat and optimistic view of tomorrow lead to better performance?

There is reason to be concerned about students whose academic performance lags behind the pack. Note the differences in Table 3.1.

Clearly, efforts to enable teenagers to excel in their academic work have some effect upon their view of themselves and their future. It may also affect their willingness to have a good relationship with family and peers and to apply themselves more aggressively to personal development.

But even more impressive than the effect of academic performance is the influence of having a sense of purpose and direction in life. Once again, compare the differences in self-description between the kids who have a defined purpose and those who do not.

TABLE 3.2		
Self-Description of Teens	Have Purpose	Do Not Have Purpose
Excited about life	89%	65%
Trusting of people	83	67
Optimistic about the future	80	64
A leader	71	49
Religious	61	47
Stressed out	33	50
Lonely	7	24
Discouraged	8	21

The relationships are very similar—the bottom line being that the more clarity of purpose, the more likely the person is to have self-worth and to be enthusiastic about the future.

Why does it matter? After more than two decades of public opinion and behavioral research, I have learned that *attitudes shape expectations*, and *expectations influence outcomes*. In other words, what you think is what you get. People who do not expect their marriages to be successful usually wind up getting divorced. People who assume that others will not like them often end up being friendless. People who do not believe in themselves are incapable of facilitating other people's belief in them. And so it will be with our young people. If young people see themselves as incapable and unlovable, chances are better than not that their lives will be marked by lack of achievement and loneliness. If they believe that the future holds little promise, they are more likely to live in a debilitating world.

Statistically, more than one-quarter of today's teenagers lack a sense of purpose or the academic achievement that marks them as good candidates for a positive future. That translates to more than 5 million kids between 13 and 17 who are already operating at a disadvantage.

Brain Power

The issue of academic performance raises yet another quandary: the literacy level and analytical ability of teenagers. In the Age of Information, where information breeds power, the capacity to read, write and reason is crucial to getting ahead or achieving personal goals.

Literacy was elevated to the national headlines recently when an extensive government study proclaimed that half of all adults in America are functionally illiterate.[3] If adults are struggling with literacy, and given the national outcry about the declining level of quality in our schools, what's the prognosis for the young regarding literacy?

In short, it's not a pretty picture. Recent studies have shown that American students are losing ground to students from other industrialized nations (most notably Germany, Japan and France). This can be traced to the fact that American high school students spend only three hours of a typical school day in classes teaching core subjects such as English, math, science, history, geography, foreign languages, civics and fine arts. In other words, of all the time a student spends in a classroom, just half of it is devoted to core subjects. One federal study referred to the situation as the "dumbing down" of secondary education. The report went on to explain that the schools are now expected by parents to take responsibility for teaching everything from personal hygiene to responsible consumerism.[4]

A report by The National Assessment for Educational Progress concluded that three-quarters of high school seniors do an hour or less of homework each night; most of them read 10 pages or less in a typical day; and large numbers of students are uncomfortable working with simple mathematical problems. Meanwhile, a Census Bureau report states that 31 percent of youths ages 12 to 14 and 35 percent of kids 15 to 17 are enrolled below their appropriate grade level or prematurely dropped out of school. Funding cutbacks have resulted in larger class sizes, which lead to less personalized attention from teachers. Textbooks have been simplified. The school year has been shortened and national standards for achievement are being resisted.

The results are predictable. Vocabulary levels of teenagers are plummeting. In a standardized vocabulary test among 18-year-olds who expect to enroll in a college the coming year, students correctly defined the test words only 30 percent of the time. That is roughly equivalent to what they would have scored through random guessing.[5] College entrance exam scores on standardized tests have been slowly declining in both math and language skills for the past three decades. Interviews we have conducted among employers suggest that teenagers represent a poorly skilled labor pool with whom it is difficult to communicate on anything but an elementary level. Students consistently show a declining ability to solve problems, to articulate a well-reasoned argument, to think conceptually and to build lasting relationships.

It has been suggested by some educational researchers, however, that we may be in a transition time in which styles of thinking are changing and the schools have not yet discovered how to capitalize on this new situation. There is evidence that the introduction of computers within the classroom and in homes is having an unintended effect on how kids collect, organize and analyze information. Some have called this a shift from a traditional "linear" style of thinking (moving from point A to point B to point C in succession to reach an organized conclusion) to a more technology-driven "parallel" or "mosaic" mode of thought (moving randomly among a series of points before integrating them into a coherent pattern and drawing a conclusion). This new form of thinking is in line with how computers organize data and how some computer games and software packages lead kids to think.

This new style may be beneficial to the emerging generation. Mosaic learning permits faster processing and a greater absorption of information than does a linear pattern. The analytic process may take longer, but the residue is a heightened possibility of creative solutions to complex problems.

THE QUESTION OF CHARACTER

All of the attributes we have discussed reflect the inner being of our youth. If they are to master their world, they will do so the same way every other successful generation in every nation has—on the strength of their character. Facts can be researched, techniques can be learned and relationships can be developed. But character is the inner quality that determines the paths they will pursue and their responses to the choices they face. Character will define teenagers and their legacy.

As we survey the character traits of teenagers, we find them to be the latest iteration in a constantly evolving breed of young people. If the teenagers of old were rather static and predictable, those since the late '80s have been continually breaking new ground. Without becoming immersed in statistics, here is what we have determined about our present crop of teens.

Teenagers respect integrity in other people, but are not willing to make the sacrifices to develop integrity in their own lives. Compared to past generations of teens, today's teens are more likely to cheat on exams, lie, loaf on the job, steal from those who have an abundance, exploit the mistakes of others rather than show compassion toward them, and avoid accepting responsibility unless they can see an advantage to embracing it. In many instances, integrity is taken to mean doing whatever furthers one's personal advantage without being caught. Teens have little sympathy and no respect for those who strive to beat the system and fail. We are not aware of any segment that has so easily embraced such concepts as the "white lie" and stealing with the intent of returning the taken goods (i.e., "permanent borrowing").

Many teens lack relational skills. Relationships are more highly esteemed by today's teens than by boomers when they were of the same age. Yet, while many teens desire deeper, lasting relationships, they do not have the communication skills, the commitment to loyalty and forgiveness and the emotional maturity to foster such bonding. One reason group activity—dating, entertainment and sports—is so popular is because it takes the onus off the individual, diverting the attention to a variety of people rather than a single individual or couple.

Teens do appreciate efforts by peers at developing true friendships and, in their own awkward ways, typically seek to maintain existing ties. People are more important than organizations, policies, structures or products to the teen; again, this conflicts with the model shown to them by their parents' generation. The death of family and friends remains one of the most frightening possibilities that lurk in the recesses of their minds.

Attention spans are shorter for teens. Channel surfing and radio scanning are common. Reading magazine articles instead of books is in. Movies on video are often interrupted for breaks. Listening to lectures (or sermons) that extend beyond 20 minutes or so is torturous. Attention levels can be improved through interactive processes.

Compassion runs hot and cold with teens. They like the concept, but struggle with the application. On the one hand, the majority desire to help the poor and needy; on the other hand, their concern wanes after a short period of time. They tend to believe that if something bad happens to a person, the person probably had it coming. Americans have historically rooted for the underdog; today's teens have little interest in losers.

Personal freedom remains a hot issue among teens. As Juliana Hatfield, the musician, who is one of the leading songwriters of the buster generation, explains, "I'm totally committed to the cause of individuality. That's the only thing I stand by: independence."[6] Many teenagers echo that sentiment. Programs that require regular attendance, close adherence to restrictive rules or living by hierarchical authority structures are avoided. Teens are not anarchists, but they do appreciate a huge degree of latitude in their lives.

Perseverance is not a trademark of today's teenagers. They live in a world of opportunities and a world defined by change. They don't hesitate to flit from option to option, sampling the alternatives and savoring the best until a better possibility emerges. (The sole exception would be in friendships; in this arena they fare better at building lasting bridges.) Their patterns of sticking with jobs are horrendous. Their commitment to causes shifts on a 9- to 12-month cycle. TV networks crave teens as an audience (because advertisers target them), but are stupefied by their irregular viewing habits. Homework problems that cannot be solved within a few minutes typically do not get solved. Saving money for the future is not their forte.

Morality remains something of an enigma to most young people. They are likely to describe themselves as moral not because of what they do, but because of how they feel. Because they believe they always try to make the right decision in any situation, most deem themselves to be moral individuals. In practice, however, they live in accordance with situational ethics and moral relativism. More than four out of five of them argue that there is not—and cannot be—such a notion as absolute moral truth. They contend that only they can determine what is right or wrong for themselves in any given situation, and that what is right or wrong for themselves may be different from the choices made by others in the same situation.

Lacking absolute standards and moral benchmarks, today's teens are constantly under the stress of having to determine (and defend) their decisions about right and wrong. Because they operate in a values vacuum, they are never comfortable about their moral decisions, but suffer with loads of personal second-guessing. In their defense, though, at least they are struggling with the question. They have been disgusted by what many of them characterize as the overt greed, human manipulation and emotional emptiness of their parents' lives. They want something better, something purer and something deeper. They're still searching.

KEEP ON BUILDING

Objectively speaking, it must be exceedingly difficult to be a teenager in the late '90s. Teenagers have to convince themselves that there is hope for the future. They are exploring a morally bankrupt culture in search of morals, values, ethics and meaning. They are the most technologically literate group of young people the nation has ever known, but they struggle to communicate what they feel, and they wrestle with decision making. The educational system has let them down, and yet they are the ones who will pay most dearly for that failure. They are worn down by stress, rushed into maturity before their time and operating without viable role models.

You cannot help but have compassion on teenagers. More power to them if they are able to persuade themselves that it is worth sticking around for the future.

Notes

1. The survey "Teenage Update 1995" was conducted through telephone interviews with 723 young adults between the ages of 13 and 18. The interviews were conducted in December 1994 and January 1995 with a random sample of these teenagers.
2. Corroboration for these views comes from some of the ongoing explorations by Barna Research among teens; studies by the Higher Education Research Institute at UCLA; and tracking studies of teenagers conducted by The George H. Gallup International Institute.
3. "Adult Literacy in America," National Center for Education Statistics, U.S. Department of Education, Washington, D.C., 1993.
4. "Education: No Time for Learning," *Newsweek*, 16 May 1994, 58.
5. "Talking with Fewer Words," *American Demographics* (April 1995): 13.
6. Jeff Giles, "Sex and the Single Songwriter," *Newsweek*, 6 September 1993, 52.

4 FRIENDS, FAMILY AND FUN

In the '50s and '60s, they said you could tell a lot about people by the company they kept. In the '70s and '80s, they said you could determine a person's priorities by the checkbook he or she kept. I contend that in the '90s, you can tell all you need to know about people by the schedule they keep. As our lifestyles and values have changed, our focus has moved from the little black book to the checkbook to the Daytimer.

What's in the figurative Daytimer of teenagers? First of all, although they are stressed out and feel pressured, they are generally not so obsessed with schedules that they actually keep a Daytimer. Such fastidious attention to scheduling is a hallmark of the baby boomers. In fact, although teens' lives are jammed with activities, understanding their lifestyle priorities becomes pretty simple: friends, music, family, TV and school just about covers it.

TWENTY-FOUR HOURS A DAY

Every day is a new adventure in the life of teenagers—new lessons, new faces, new heartbreaks, new crises and new victories. Yet, a fairly predictable series of activities defines their way of life.

Most teens sleep about eight hours each night. Upon waking, an hour or so is consumed in preparation for the coming day: they shower, dress, engage in grooming rituals and wolf down breakfast. The following seven hours are spent in school activity.

After school, real life begins. Three to four hours may be spent hanging out with friends—less than that if the teenager has a job that requires his or her presence for several hours after school. (The older the teen, the more likely a part-time job is held, compressing the time with confidants.)

In terms of the life priorities of teens, their friends are definitely at the top of the list. More than three out of every four teens revealed they spend at least two hours each day interacting with their friends. Sometimes the interaction is roaming the malls, sometimes it's sitting in a fast-food joint eating a burger together. Often it includes brief slots of time shared during the school day (lunches, breaks, study halls); occasionally it is engaging in a sports contest. Wherever and whenever it occurs, these links are vital to the sense of fulfillment teens squeeze out of their day.

But media exposure also plays a key role in the after-school agenda. The typical teen will devote almost two hours a day to viewing TV and another two hours or so listening to music on the radio or from recordings (audiotapes, CDs). Either or both of these endeavors are likely to take place while the teen is completing his or her one hour of homework.

This is a substantial change from the past. Homework consumes less of the free time of teenagers than it used to. By some accounts, teens formerly devoted an average of three hours an evening to preparing for the coming school day. The decrease in time spent on homework is not because today's kids are so much brighter than those of years gone by, but because the schools have become less demanding and many of them provide time during the school day to complete assignments. Many analysts observe that teens could use a larger dose of homework to push them academically, but that the schools have dramatically relaxed their expectations.

The typical teenager, incidentally, will allocate roughly one-quarter of his or her TV attention—that's about 25 minutes a day—to MTV. Somewhere in the mix, the youth might read something that is not required for school, putting in about a half an hour on such extracurricular reading. Throw in a half hour for dinner and the day is complete.

A few other passing revelations might be of interest. Most teenagers use a computer during the average day. They are likely to use a computer for about 30 to 40 minutes daily. For many kids, this means a school-owned personal computer (PC); for a growing number, however, it might be time invested on a home PC. The typical teen spends more time on a computer than on nonrequired reading or watching MTV.

KIDS WANT THEIR MTV

And what about MTV, the music channel that has forever changed both television and young people? To some observers, MTV is a tool of the devil; to others, it is an indispensable window into our culture. The truth may be somewhere in between.

As far as teenagers are concerned, MTV is just cool entertainment. Few of them see it in the ominous or grandiose terms assigned to it by some religious leaders and conservative analysts. Instead, they think of it as music and slice-of-life video tailored to the interests of their generation, in the same way that ESPN, American Movie Classics or other niched cable networks pander to the tastes of their parents. Teenagers do not think of MTV as an educational channel; they think of it as a satisfying filler.

Kids of all stripes watch MTV. Unlike many cable channels, which draw heavily from specific demographic segments, MTV pulls its audience rather evenly from all of the teen population subgroups: white, nonwhite, male, female, liberal, conservative, affluent and economically marginal. Several segments of the teen mass are more inclined to watch the channel and for longer periods of time: kids under 16, teens who attend a Catholic Church and those who are most addicted to media of any kind (i.e., those who spend above-average amounts of time listening to radio, using their stereo, watching TV, or reading books and magazines).

MTV is not watched in the same way other channels are watched, however. Because its predominant format is three- to four-minute video clips, teens tend to watch several videos, then flip to another channel. Relatively few watch the network for an extended time period, unless they are viewing the serial programming (such as *Beavis and Butthead* or *The Real World*).

Although there is no research to confirm it, MTV has probably had as great an influence on teenagers as any other television programming. The primary influence seems to have been the channel's ability to redefine teenagers' expectations of television programming, to reshape their attention spans, to present them with new ideas about society and relationships, and to confirm the acceptability of certain perspectives and behaviors. The channel has also given life (and a platform) to new cultural icons. Madonna, Peter Gabriel and Janet Jackson are among the circle of idolized and influential performers who might not have had an audience without the push their careers received from MTV.

From our research, however, no statistical correlation exists between some of the high-profile, at-risk behaviors and viewing MTV. For instance, kids who do not watch MTV are just as likely to use drugs as kids who do watch the channel. Teenagers who do not watch MTV have virtually the same probability of engaging in sexual intercourse as do the kids who include MTV in the TV diet. The kids who are most heavily involved in religious activities or who have made a commitment to Christ are just as likely as their irreligious peers to have regular exposure to the vilified music channel. Although perceptions and behavior may well be influenced in some important ways by what kids see on the channel, no statistical information is available to date that shows that MTV is culpable for the bad decisions some of our kids make.

In fact, there is another way of looking at the data on MTV viewing by teenagers. Kids who are born-again Christians, those who attend church regularly and those whose families are most religious are just as likely to watch MTV as kids who are not Christian, those who avoid church and those who come from families that ignore the spiritual dimension. Further, the data reveal that there is no relationship between a teenager's perceptions about moral truth and their viewing habits of MTV.

My point is not to defend MTV as a beacon of morality and family values. The channel indisputably has a negative effect on the minds and the behaviors of our young people. However, its influence is possible only because of the vacuum in the lives of young people that is no longer filled by family, church and school. As these three institutions have surrendered aspects of their historical responsibilities in developing young people's values, perspectives and lifestyles, something inevitably had to emerge to fill that gap.

MTV did not create a need. It simply filled an existing hole with one alternative. Being the first to market usually earns the early bird the largest share of the market.

SPORTS INVOLVEMENT

Teenagers also remain in tune with sports, particularly professional sports. Although health surveys report that our kids have become flabbier and less healthy during the past decade and a half, this is a response to different lifestyles rather than a reflection of declining interest in traditional athletics.

When my generation was growing up, the most popular sports for teenagers were team sports: Baseball, basketball and football were the big three. Schools provided opportunities for organized games during gym class, free periods and after school. Just as often, though, those of us who had organizational skills—or a telephone—would bring together a group of peers for a loosely organized but brutally competitive game.

Times have changed. Schools have suffered budget cuts and therefore offer fewer opportunities for intramural sports. Newly constructed schools include less extensive athletic facilities. Kids live in homes that have smaller yards and therefore have less access to space in which to have their amateur contests. Millions of kids fear playing without adult supervision because of the potential for interruptions by roaming gangs. And trying to pull together a group large enough to sustain a basketball game is difficult; corralling enough kids to play football, baseball or soccer is very difficult, given the schedules of teens (and their chauffeuring mothers).

Traditional wisdom maintains that sports are useful tools for teaching kids teamwork, conflict resolution and other transferable skills. Increasingly, however, scheduling and other realities of life in the '90s make sports less of an educational or character-building tool than a conditioning mechanism. Consider the sports that garner the most widespread participation among teenagers: swimming, bicycling, basketball, camping and bowling. With the exception of basketball, these are solo endeavors. Only one out of every five teenagers engages in football, softball, baseball or volleyball team sports during the year.[1] Many schools are offering teenagers electives that enable them to choose the sport or athletic endeavors they will participate in, and team sports seem to be losing ground.

WHAT ABOUT FAMILY TIME?

A glaring omission in the time capsule of teenagers is the time spent with family. My failure to include family time in the typical calendar of teens is not an oversight. Teenagers noted that they spend incredibly little time with their family during the week. It is becoming less common these days for a teenager to have time isolated for focused interaction with family members. Most of the time they spend with their family is what you might call "family and" time: family and TV, family and dinner, family and homework, etc. The lives of each family member are usually so jam-packed that the opportunity to spend time together doing unique activities—talking about life, visiting special places, playing games and sharing spiritual explorations—has to be scheduled in advance. Few do so.

No Time for Talking

A wonderful but unfortunate example of this concerns how much time teenagers and their parents spend in what the teen considers to be meaningful conversation. Although the average has risen in the past decade, time devoted to such talks is amazingly minuscule. On average, teens say they devote about two hours a week discussing things that are important to them with their mothers, and just one hour a week discussing meaningful matters with their fathers. To put this into proper context, realize that teenagers now spend more time watching television in a typical day than they spend interacting with their fathers during an entire week. They allocate more of their attention to eating, grooming and using personal computers than they do to communicating seriously with their parents. The human beings who get the greatest amount of their reflective time are not parents but their friends.

For those who worry (rightfully so) that we are raising a generation whose values have been implanted and nurtured by ignorant, immoral or impersonal forces, this has happened largely because parents have unwittingly defaulted on their traditional roles as values progenitors. Our research shows that the problem is not the teenagers: they are open to, if not hoping for, more time committed to serious conversations and relationship-building experiences with their parents. The tyranny of the busy schedule has precluded the growth of the easy and frequent communication that millions of teens crave—despite their hardened and challenging exterior. Teens do not beg for attention. They believe that if they want to become independent, they must learn to master reality on their own terms, in their own way. Receiving counsel from Mom and Dad would be valued, but it seems to teens that the only people truly concerned about parental guidance are the movie studios whose films are rated by the Motion Picture Association of America.

Missing in Action

Almost one-third of today's teenagers are being raised in households in which only one of their natural parents is present. Divorce, perhaps the most pervasive and pernicious legacy of the '60s and '70s, has ravaged the American family. Most kids whose parents divorce wind up living with their mothers (only about 15 percent live with their fathers). A majority of the divorced moms who remarry eventually get divorced again, complicating things even further for their children.

Analysts have found that kids are better off in a home in which the parents tolerate each other than they are in a single-parent family or a remarriage environment. The absence of both natural parents has been shown to have devastating effects on kids. A child growing up in a home in which one or both natural parents is absent is more likely to—in contrast to kids from intact families—receive less parental attention; receive less discipline; be less adept at playing with peers; have more frequent and more serious health problems, more frequently exhibit emotional problems, sexual problems and antisocial behavior.

Such a child is more likely than the norm to get divorced; is more pessimistic about the future; lacks role models; is more likely to experience bouts of depression and a deep sense of loneliness and rejection; is more likely to commit crimes; and also struggles with low self-esteem, anger, guilt and lower levels of achievement.[2]

A government study among kids from broken families showed they are more likely to be expelled or suspended from school and to repeat a grade in school.[3] Gary Collins, a Christian psychologist, has reported that mental illness is one of the most devastating outgrowths of family division. His research shows that four out of every five adolescents in psychiatric hospitals come from broken homes.[4] Although the adults going through a divorce experience a spectrum of emotional challenges, endure financial hardships and have other serious issues to overcome, it may be the children of the broken union who suffer the most damage.

One of the most disheartening realizations is that a majority of teens living with stepfathers say they spend no time at all during the week in meaningful conversations with their surrogate dads. The situation is not as dire among the youth who live with stepmothers: just 17 percent say they have no time in meaningful communication with their stepmothers. In both cases, however, the proportion of teens who do not talk meaningfully with their stepparents is more than double the proportion found among kids whose natural families are intact.

Family Activities

What does family time look like for contemporary teenagers? In short, it's inconsistent and somewhat unpredictable. It contains a pinch of spirituality; a dash of confrontation and resolution; an occasional meal out or attending a game; and infrequent forays into the realm of values, morals and ethics.

During a typical week, about half of all teenagers attend church services with their families and about half will become involved in discussions about family problems or disagreements between parents and children.

On two or three occasions during a typical month, teenagers will pray with family members (often a blessing at mealtime); go out to a restaurant for a meal together; discuss something related to their religious views or experiences; and talk about issues that address morals, ethics and personal values.

It is rather uncommon for teens to play games with family members. This seems to happen because of teens' pride ("I'm too old for that now") rather than the unwillingness of parents to give it a try. Of the activities we evaluated, by far the least likely was to read the Bible with their families. Only 4 out of 10 teenagers ever share that experience with their families (and for some of them it takes place at church).

Does this pattern fit the mental ideal of teens? Yes—and no. The light involvement in religious activity suits them just fine because many of them do not embrace the same religious views as their folks do. Teenagers are motivated to explore spiritual reality, but many of them resent having to accept their parents' religious faiths or churches as the appropriate spiritual incubator for themselves. "I can tell what's right from what's wrong for me," intoned one disenchanted 16-year-old who gets dragged along to her mother's Presbyterian church several Sundays a month. "I've heard their pitch, seen their lifestyles, and I don't want anything more to do with that church. It's not for me. Sure, I believe in God and all, but there are better ways of being religious. It's not like I'm giving up on God, I just want to discover Him in my own way."

Discussions of family issues is a euphemism for arguments—and teens are not inordinately interested in having more of those confrontations. "Look, the deck's stacked," a 17-year-old male noted. "I can't win, by definition. If we're having a discussion, it's because mom's ticked about something I did. I can explain my side of the story, but it just fills time—it's just my role in the script. It's how the game is played: I live, she shouts, I lose."

Many teenagers believe that if their parents would truly hear their sides of the story, such discussions could be productive. The usual scenario—problem identified by parent, explanation offered by teen, explanation rejected by parent, proper solution described by parent, threat of restrictions if solution posed by parent is ignored—has run thin for most teens. Perhaps that is why a recent survey of teens discovered that the TV family they believe most resembles their own is that of the show *Roseanne*—the working-class, terminally cynical fivesome that has topped the ratings race on the strength of sarcasm and intolerance.

Even discussions about morals, values, beliefs and lifestyles grates on teens. The problem is not that they do not want to discuss these matters—they do. The conflict is that they want a real discussion, not a lecture. Teenagers believe they have wisdom beyond their years; their generation believes their value as human beings is largely reflected in the amount of input they are allowed in decision-making situations. This perspective goes beyond the usual teen rebellion against authority. They define respect and dignity in terms of the platform they are freely given to air their views.

More than earlier generations, teenagers in the '90s are aggressively challenging assumptions and actively searching for intelligent responses to difficult realities. They are not so much opposed to the positions held by their parents as they are insulted and turned off by the dictatorial approach used by many parents in communicating or promoting those positions.

One girl said, "You know, over the last few years I've gone head to head with my parents constantly." This 17-year-old girl was an A student and active in her church group. Yet, her parents had been at war with her about issue after issue for the past five years. Their home life was tense; she was anxious to go to college. "Looking back," she said, "I guess I actually agree with most of what they believe. But it would have been so much easier and faster if they had talked about these things with me, rather than imposed their views on me, as if theirs is the only possible way to do things. I'm sure they mean well, and parenting must be hard, but it's hard growing up, too. If they had been more understanding and listened more, we could have had the same results a lot sooner and with a lot less stress and anger."

GOOD KIDS, BAD CHOICES

Granted, millions of teenagers engage in at-risk behaviors. More than 600,000 teenage girls get pregnant each year; more than 9 out of 10 of those girls are unmarried; half of them terminate their pregnancies by having abortions.[5] Almost 2 million juveniles are arrested each year—and one-third of them will wind up being arrested again.[6] Suicide, theft, gambling, smoking, drinking and drugs—millions of incidents of teenagers making bad choices occur every week.

But these are not bad kids at heart. Our research shows that almost half of them (46 percent) had volunteered some of their free time during the past three months to help needy people. The older the teenagers, the more likely they are to devote some of themselves to helping others in this way. And the sense of civic responsibility is even more acute among teens from affluent homes, those who are religiously inclined and those who are among the top students.

Relatively few admit to having engaged in theft during the past quarter (only 7 percent); flipping through a pornographic magazine (7 percent); or using an illegal, nonprescription drug (8 percent). Although any teenagers engaging in these behaviors is too many, these figures are far from epidemic in proportion.

If we extend the time frame, though, to find out what kinds of at-risk behaviors teenagers have ever engaged in, the picture changes. Consider these findings:

- A quarter million teens have brought loaded guns to school.
- Nearly 1.5 million teenagers have tried unsuccessfully to commit suicide.
- About 27 percent of high school kids have had sexual intercourse—including a majority of all 18-year-olds.
- About 29 percent have consumed a sufficient quantity of alcohol to be drunk at least once in their lives.
- Four out of ten 13- to 17-year-olds have watched an X-rated or pornographic movie.

The portrait is one of a generation of young adults adrift amid a sea of appealing but harmful alternatives. Lacking a clear values system to which they are unswervingly committed, and without the trusted, compassionate and reasoned voices of their parents helping them navigate the treacherous waters of youth, many of them make bad choices. Some of those unfortunate decisions may serve as a relatively harmless lesson that builds their resolve for the future. Other experiences, however—such as sexual intercourse—may have long-term effects that leave them scared and scarred.

THE PREFERRED LIFESTYLE

The teenage years are, as they have always been, a time of paradox. Teenagers would like to have more structure provided, but without having their independence or their freedom to experiment impeded. They want to learn from the experiences and wisdom of their parents, but they're not willing to allow their elders the latitude to impart those lessons in a manner that fits parents' needs and styles. They struggle with the effects of stress, but they continue to book busy schedules. More time in intimate experiences with family would be appreciated, but they will neither push for nor create those opportunities. They are frightened by the potential consequences of many at-risk behaviors, yet they flirt with those dangers regularly.

So what do teenagers want as their ideal lifestyle? It's simple, really.

A loving, caring, listening family that balances freedom and structure, trust and rules.

A church that makes God real, makes religion fun, provides them with a chance to find truths that are comprehensible and relevant, and does not strangle them with a list of "don'ts."

Friends who are understanding and giving, who share the emotional realities of life and who can be counted on to grow with them.

Schools that require little or no homework, teach pertinent subjects in interesting ways with minimal academic pressure, and that prepare them for meaningful and exciting careers.

A schedule filled with entertaining elements: music, video imagery and a celebration of the good things in life.

The chance to make a difference without being emotionally drained or having to invest too much time.

A taste of the pleasures of life that are forbidden to minors—sex, drugs, booze and gambling—without paying the price for their dalliance with disaster.

The resources to live comfortably, without guilt or remorse, and to enjoy the best the world has to offer without becoming slaves to affluence.

As the Rolling Stones sang a quarter century ago, "You can't always get what you want...but if you try, sometimes, you can get what you need."

Notes
1. From a survey of 10,000 households conducted by the National Sporting Goods Association, supplying data on kids 12 to 17 years old. Published in the *Statistical Abstract of the United States—1994*, U.S. Department of Commerce, Bureau of the Census, U.S.G.P.O., Washington, D.C., 1994, Table 406.
2. Some of the studies that have been most insightful are described by Judith Wallerstein and Sandra Blakeslee, *Second Chances* (New York: Ticknor & Fields, 1989); Arlene Skolnick and Jerome Skolnick, *Families in Transition* (Glenview, Ill.: Scott, Foresman & Co., sixth edition, 1989); and Barbara Defoe Whitehead, "Dan Quayle Was Right," *Atlantic Monthly* (April 1993): 47-48.
3. This information was taken from a study conducted by the National Center for Health Statistics, reported in *American Demographics* (February 1992): 13.
4. From "Pastor to Pastor," a newsletter from Focus on the Family, Colorado Springs (April 1993): 2.
5. *Statistical Abstract of the United States—1994*, Tables 100, 112.
6. "Database," *U.S. News & World Report*, 20 June 1994, 14.

5 FIGHTING FOR, WITH AND ABOUT FAMILY

For several millennia, the views of teenagers about family have baffled the human race. The perspectives of young people when it comes to family are often paradoxical. They love their parents, but they can't wait to leave them. They want to be loved by their parents, but behave in ways that virtually dare anybody to love them. They wish they had more close family experiences, yet they schedule themselves away from their families as often as possible. They believe in marriage and family, but want a family that is different from the one in which they were raised. They concur that the family is a crucial foundation for a strong society, yet they have altered their concept of a viable family to reflect relationships that cannot serve as a consistent and reliable foundation.

Don't lose sight of the fact that teenagers, in spite of all the problems and difficulties they have seen and experienced in family situations, have become major proponents of family. As they look to the future, they believe the nation needs strong families; they want strong families; and conditions may be right for the resurgence of functional families.

THE IMPACT OF THE FAMILY

The teen years are marked by a seemingly endless trail of crises, major questions, contradictions and disappointments. Whether the subject relates to sexuality, money, relationships, career, school achievement, global politics or any other matter that is likely to challenge a teen, there is never a dearth of critical topics that arise and require a significant response by youth.

Like other humans, teenagers tend to react to life's challenges in light of the counsel and encouragement they receive from other people. Microsoft may get the credit for initiating interactive products, but God originated the interactive concept. He designed us to be connected, interdependent beings. Teenagers are a terrific example of the need that resides deep within each of us—granted, deeper for some than others—for instruction, correction, affirmation and direction from other people as they attempt to victoriously juggle the blitzkrieg of daily obstacles and opportunities.

Moms, Dads and Heroes

What is most interesting, though, is whom the teens of our day turn to for reliable and useful guidance. Tops on the list, by a wide margin, is Mom. Three-quarters of all teens said if they had an important question about life, Mom would be among the handful of "must see" advisers. About half of the teen population would also consult their best friends, and half said they would probably consult their fathers. The only other potential counselors to receive honorable mention status were siblings, other relatives (mostly grandparents) and trusted school teachers—each of whom was listed by 10 to 15 percent of the teens as likely sources of wisdom and influence.

This result is sobering for mothers. Clearly, they have a huge responsibility when it comes to mentoring their kids. Although mothers often have the most intense confrontations with their teenagers—and that is generally because it is the mother, not the father, who serves as the dominant disciplinarian—moms remain the most trusted ally of their teens when push comes to shove. Moms and their teens might be at odds about lifestyle, values or perspective, but those divisions are quickly forgotten when the teen needs solace, wisdom or support. Moms are therefore in a vulnerable position: although their views may be challenged, their words and actions possess power and significance in the minds of their maturing kids.

Mothers are most likely to remain the most important counselor in the life of a teen throughout the teenage years. In contrast, the status of Dad as an adviser wanes as time passes. Among 13-year-olds, 6 out of 10 said their father would be one of the few people they'd turn to with a major life question. By the time the child is 18, Dad is still in the inner circle among just 1 out of every 4! This reflects the growing tension and distance between teens and fathers as the kids age and as the struggles the teens face become more complex and more time consuming.

Yet another expression of influence is evident in the heroes of teenagers. Although most of them assert that heroes are important, a large proportion of them do not have people they look up to. Many of the teenagers who have heroes name entertainers and athletes. Among the individuals whom the teenagers actually know personally, however, mothers and fathers were those whose lives the young people would most like to imitate.

It is worth noting that when teens think of the people who influence their lives or the people who serve as role models and heroes, not one religious leader is included in the top 20. Michael Jordan is watched and listened to more carefully than is Billy Graham or Josh McDowell. Charles Barkley defeats Charles Colson in the influence derby. The local radio or TV personality is more likely to have widespread influence among teenagers than their pastors or youth group leaders. It is not that religion is unimportant to teens; rather, few of them look upon the religious leaders they know as being worthy of respect and imitation.

What Is Family?

But we cannot lose sight of the fact that we are operating in an era of history when many of the fundamental institutions and relationships that shaped our nation are being questioned. For instance, Americans have traditionally described "family" as all of the people who are related to each other by marriage, birth or adoption. No longer is this the prevailing definition. Several years ago, we discovered that a majority of adults now define family to be any and all individuals whom they deeply care for or who deeply care about them.[1]

Not surprisingly, teenagers have now adopted the same perspective. Almost two out of three teens currently believe that this nouveau definition of family is the most accurate. They contend that it does not exclude individuals who are related by blood or marriage from being deemed family, but it does not automatically give them such preferred status. In other words, in our achievement-oriented society, there are no more free rides—if you want to be part of the family, you have to earn that right.

This new definition of family is frightening. It renders the family a fluid and transitory aggregation, based upon the emotion of the moment and the most recent experiences individuals have had with each other. Considering this view of family, the people who represent your family today may not be considered your family tomorrow by virtue of changes in emotion, experience, peer pressure or other whims.

We have also detected that one unfortunate outgrowth of the new family is that behaviors that have traditionally been discouraged—divorce, cohabitation, births without marriage, extramarital affairs, even polygamy—become acceptable to some. Because the definition of a family permits anyone and everyone to share emotions, housing and intimate relationships, it becomes a "family on the fly" existence in which family, like everything else in our culture, exists only to gratify our immediate needs without regard for long-term consequences.

Parents, in particular, seem lost when seeking to address this new family concept. They are pleased that family is meaningful to their young adults, but how do they effectively restore a more conventional view of who or what constitutes a family? This is not a minor matter either, for until parents (or other respected authority figures) succeed at changing the definition, the chances are slim that their moral, ethical, spiritual or cultural arguments will effectively dissuade their youngsters from engaging in cohabitation, promiscuous sexuality, single parenthood and the like.

Evidence of Confusion

Our research also points out that in spite of their willingness to expound upon their family beliefs, many teens aren't really sure what they believe about family. Their opinions and family philosophy are riddled with contradictions and undermined by silent doubts. Most teens argue that God intended marriage to last for a lifetime, yet they contend that a rocky marriage should not be maintained just because children are involved. Four out of five teenagers say they enjoy being at home with their families, but then they modify that by stating that they prefer to spend their free time with friends, the media or attending entertainment events.

A majority of teens believe that marriage is a viable institution and assert that they hope to be married some day, but most of them also hedge their bets by cautioning that it is very hard to have a successful marriage these days. And although two out of three teens say they want marriages like those of their parents, most of them rate their parents' marriages to be only moderately healthy.

Why are teens confused? Because they have heard traditional perspectives about family shared by parents, church leaders and other influencers, but they are not encouraged by the kind of family conditions those views have produced in reality. In fact, although two-thirds of all adults believe that "if the traditional family falls apart, American society will collapse," only half of all teenagers buy this notion. Yes, they want family—close-knit, relational, supportive, functional family—but they are open to new structures and means of achieving such a relational unit. Teenagers are all too aware of nasty divorces, heartbreaking affairs, physical abuse and the emotional detachment between spouses that spoil millions of families. They are determined to have a more harmonious and fulfilling family life than their parents enjoyed, but they are not persuaded that embracing the same underlying values their parents have will facilitate the superior family life they crave.

THE FUNCTIONAL FAMILY

As teenagers think about their own future families, they have rather traditional expectations, even if the path to getting there may be a bit nontraditional. Consider, for instance, the following facts.

Sex and Marriage
Although teens get branded as sex-crazed, their perceptions of the value and benefits of marriage are not driven by society's approval of marriage as the institution in which sex is permitted. Among the 16- to 18-year-olds in America, having satisfying sexual relationships with their partners is not one of the highest rated goals in their lives! Life conditions such as good health, having comfortable lifestyles, identifying meaningful purposes for living, having close friends and having single marital partners for life outranked the desirability of satisfying sex lives with their marriage partners as top priorities for their future.

Part of the reason sex is no longer such a driving influence in the decision to marry is that the vast majority of married adults will either have had sex with each other or with other people prior to marriage. The bottom line in America is that sex is no longer a motivation for getting married.

Spouse and Kids
In past generations, as many as 9 out of 10 teens expressed a desire to have a spouse and kids. The coming battalion of parents are less eager to be in a family way. Although 97 percent of them said they are very or somewhat likely to get married, and government statistics estimate that about 80 to 85 percent will actually do so, just 7 out of 10 said they consider it very desirable to have children. Implication: The smaller family sizes of the past two decades are likely to remain in effect.

Long-Term Marriage
Eight out of 10 teens said that having the same marriage partner for life would be very desirable to them. This breaks with the conventional wisdom that emphasizes the absence of commitment and loyalty in the lives and relationships of young people these days. The fact is, having the same

spouse for life is viewed as a laudable achievement, as a means to a more pleasing life, as a way of enhancing the lives of their children and as a reflection of the conservative social values that many teens possess. (Teens are twice as likely to characterize their social and political ideology as conservative than to describe it as liberal.)

Sex Outside of Marriage

What makes the journey to this traditional marital state so treacherous is the behaviors they are likely to engage in along the way:

More than four out of five kids (82 percent) have had sexual relations with a member of the opposite sex by the age of 19. This means that prior to marriage, most young adults will have had sex with others and less than one-fifth of newlyweds will be virgins.[2]

Before they even graduate from high school, one-fifth of all students will have had at least four sex partners. One consequence of this promiscuity is that more than 1 million teenagers are likely to contract a sexually transmitted disease this year.[3]

If current trends continue, *a majority of today's high school students will live with a partner prior to getting married.* In a large proportion of those situations, the cohabitants will not marry each other, although they will have sexual relations with each other many times before dissolving the relationship.

Sure, teens will age and marry, and most will have one or two children, but divorce will likely wreak havoc on many of the formal unions. We can expect to see millions of children born to single parents and others born to cohabiting parents.

Family Time

The previous chapter noted that typical parents spend little time during the week involved in meaningful conversation with their teenagers. Yet parents claim they do spend time—both quality time and quantity time—with their teens. So just what do they do together?

Among the activities the family is most likely to do together are discussing family problems and attending church. On average, teens told us that each of these corporate endeavors occurs about once a week. Praying together, sharing a meal at a restaurant and discussing their religious faith, values and ethical issues are exercises that take place two or three times a month. Playing games together is a monthly experience. The family rarely, if ever, reads the Bible together.

The religious experience of the family is worth studying in greater detail. The research reveals that about half of all teenagers attend church services each week. Very few teens whose families do not attend a church make the pilgrimage on their own. Teens may be inclined to explore spirituality, but they are not nearly as prone to regularly attend church if the decision of whether or not to go is left up to them.

The prayer life of the family is also rather thin. Although one out of five teenagers prays with the family on a typical day, most of those are mealtime prayers. It is relatively uncommon for a teen to pray any type of extended, substantive prayer with his or her family other than in thanksgiving for food. And one of the least common activities of all is for families to read or study the Bible together. One out of every four teenagers will do so at least once a week. Based on other studies we have conducted, it is feasible that even that figure is an overestimation of how often the family reads the Bible together.

The encouraging news, however, is that even if most teens and their families do not frequently engage in traditional religious activities, there is at least some ongoing, if irregular, dialogue about spiritual matters. One out of every nine teenagers lives in a home in which religious matters are discussed on a daily basis. Another one in eight is from a family that discuss these matters two or three times a week, and one out of six tackles the topic weekly. We do not know the nature, the depth or the impact of those discussions. The fact that religion becomes a viable topic for consideration, however, is cause for celebration.

The research shows that the older teens are, the less likely they are to participate in family discussions about faith matters. In fact, kids who are 13 and 14 years old are twice as likely as older teens to engage in religious discussions with their families. Our studies also found that if teenagers do not discuss religious affairs at home, they are much less likely to raise these matters with their friends. The teens who rarely or never had religious discussions with family were three times less likely than those who do have such conversations to interact on faith matters with their peers.

Family Spirituality Matters

For critics who contend that exposure to religious education and faith training makes no difference in the lives of young people, the facts indisputably argue otherwise. As it turns out, one of the most powerful positive influences upon a teen's behavior was the involvement, with family, in spiritual activities and discussions.

We learned that when a teenager's family involves the teen in religious endeavors, the teen has a different lifestyle and mind-set. Here are some of the correlations between family spirituality and teen behaviors and attitudes.

Church attendance. In families that regularly attend church together, teens are more likely to be optimistic about the future, volunteer to help the needy, want to make a difference with their lives, and engage in every form of religious activity we evaluated (e.g., praying daily, attending a church group each week, attending a Bible study group every week, attending Sunday School or Catechism weekly and reading the Bible each week). They are less likely than teenagers who do not attend church to steal, view pornography, use drugs, have sexual intercourse, get drunk and define the purpose of life as enjoyment and personal fulfillment.

Praying together. Teenagers whose families pray together during the week are more likely to be optimistic about the future, volunteer to help the needy, want to make a difference with their lives and engage in every form of religious activity we evaluated. They are less likely than teenagers who do not pray with their families each week to view pornography, use drugs, have sexual intercourse, get drunk and attempt suicide.

Bible reading. If teens come from families that read the Bible together at least once a week they are more likely than other teens to want their lives to make a difference and to engage in all of the other forms of religious involvement we tested. They are less likely than teenagers whose families do not read the Bible together to steal from others, view pornography, use drugs, have sexual intercourse and get drunk.

Faith discussions. Teens who discuss their faith at least once a week with their families are more likely than other kids to be optimistic about the future, volunteer to help the needy, want to make a difference with their lives and engage in every form of religious activity we studied. They are less likely than teenagers who do not discuss faith issues with their families each week to view pornography, use drugs, have sexual intercourse, get drunk and perceive the purpose of life to be enjoyment and personal fulfillment.

Although this is encouraging news, let me caution you not to take it too far. Because of the nature of such research we cannot tell which conditions cause which responses. Consequently, we don't know if teenagers who exhibit more laudable lifestyles and attitudes do so because their families are more spiritual, or if their families are more spiritually inclined because of the positive influence of the teen, or if these teens harbor better values and behaviors because their families simply do a better job at parenting and nurturing them (regardless of religious involvement). The first explanation seems the most likely, but it cannot be proven from this research. We can definitely say, however, that there is a positive relationship between family spirituality and positive teen behaviors and attitudes.

Notes

1. See George Barna, *The Future of the American Family* (Chicago: Moody Press, 1993), chap. 2.
2. Guttmacher Institute, reported in *Youthworker Update* (September 1994): 4.
3. Data released by the Centers for Disease Control, reported in *National & International Religion Report*, 13 January 1992, 8, and 20 April 1992, 7; and Susan Brink, "Doctors for Teenagers," *U.S. News & World Report*, 16 May 1994, 77-78.

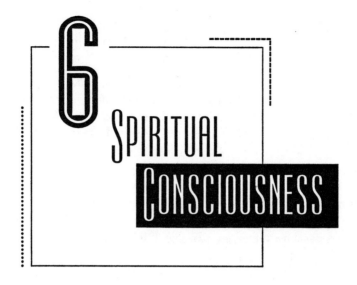

6 SPIRITUAL CONSCIOUSNESS

I recently had a revealing discussion with the senior pastor of a Protestant church. To his credit, he had realized that it is important to expose young people to Christianity, reaching them with Christian truths and principles before they leave home after high school. His church, to its credit, shared the pastor's belief on the importance of youth ministry and allocated a substantial share of the church's annual budget to ministry among kids. Clearly, the intentions were praiseworthy. Now, after several years of high-energy youth ministry and church-wide support for outreach to young people, the pastor was perplexed by his church's documented failure to attract and influence high schoolers.

"I don't get it," he said. "We structured the youth program around their tastes. On Wednesdays we give them loud, fast guitar music, we use videos, they play silly games, and we limit the teaching to a brief but powerful inspection of a useful biblical truth. They get the gospel in words and settings that are meaningful to them. Same thing on Sundays, where we've created an alternative experience for them so they don't have to deal with the adult services.

"We have a young guy on staff—bright, energetic, seminary grad, someone who is in tune with their world. He dresses like them, talks like them, is always accessible to them. He really cares about these kids—they're his life. I guess we just overestimated how spiritual kids are these days. I thought they'd really resonate with the style of ministry we developed in response to their tastes and preferences."

The Puzzle of Teen Spirituality

This conversation may be the most recent I've had with a church leader who is baffled by teens, but it is far from a unique conversation. Church leaders all over the nation are stymied. There is no doubt that churches such as the one described have a real heart for loving teens into God's presence. I shudder to think where the nation would be without such havens of truth and love for teens.

But let's get some perspective. Attracting kids to church does require relevance in style, but it is not the performance itself that will cause them to embrace Christ and His Church. If kids want a show, better venues and more professional performers are available. If they want hot music, MTV and FM radio serve it up 24 hours a day. Having a separate, stylized Sunday morning experience is very thoughtful and probably the most appropriate way of appealing to kids, but no matter how great the church service may be, sleeping in would be preferable. Kids respond to people who care about them, but when we dress like them they're as likely to be suspicious as they are comforted. Remember, being part of a church is not among their top goals in life.

But the most crucial point is that teenagers these days *are* highly "spiritual," but they are not very *religious*, nor are they naturally inclined to embrace *Christianity* as their faith of choice. They are, after all, the first generation of Americans to be raised without the culturally established assumption that they would start their religious explorations with Christianity and continue to seek a faith system only if Christianity was found wanting.

The belief system maintained by most teenagers is a combination of Christianity, pragmatism, Far Eastern traditions and utilitarianism. They are not opposed to Christianity. They simply see no compelling reason to choose one faith system over another if they don't have to. Why not take the best from each faith group they're exposed to and combine those valued elements into a comfortable, customized religious smorgasbord? This does not mean they are not spiritual. On the contrary, they are more spiritual than boomers ever were. They simply explore, discuss, consider, embrace and live out faith matters differently than did their predecessors.

Aren't We All Christians?

Several years ago, I wrote that the notion of being a Christian had been genericized by Americans. We have largely removed the biblical connotations from the term to the point where being a Christian is now synonymous with being an American. Just as "Kleenex" is used to refer to tissues, "a Xerox" to mean a photocopy, or "Scotch Tape" to describe a type of adhesive, so "Christian" means for most Americans that you are a citizen of the greatest nation on earth.

Not surprisingly, most teenagers call themselves Christian. Nationwide, almost 9 out of 10 young adults (86 percent) use the term "Christian" to describe their spiritual preference. Like their parents, however, they use this term without assigning moral or ethical content to it; in fact, they pretty much use the word by default. After all, what else would they call themselves?

The bankruptcy of the term itself is demonstrated by how few teenagers ascribe true value to the substance behind the label. Less than half of all teenagers (42 percent) claim that the Christian faith is very important in their lives today. At the same time, fewer than one out of every five teens claim that Christianity is not at all important in their daily existence.

Thus, for a large mass of young people, Christianity is of some importance though certainly not of central significance. This fits with their perspectives that faith—but not necessarily a single faith perspective—is crucial to their health, welfare and happiness as human beings. More than two-thirds more teenagers assert that spirituality and their religious beliefs are of great importance in their lives than contend that Christianity is of such lofty significance.

This also corresponds with the fact that four out of five teenagers say the Christian faith is relevant to their lives. Indeed, any philosophy that provides tips on successful living or guides them toward greater purpose and meaning is relevant to them. But just as most teenagers prefer watching a video to reading a book, few of them would go as far as to suggest that books are therefore worthless. Likewise, the Christian faith is relevant to most teenagers, but they do not feel compelled to accept every iota of Christian doctrine to receive the benefit of its relevance.

Teenagers appreciate Christianity. However, it is simply one of the streams of ethical, moral and religious thought that feed the river of religious perspectives they possess.

WHO OR WHAT IS GOD?

The breadth of openness teenagers have regarding their faith claims is amply demonstrated by their reactions to core Christian tenets. Take the way they think about God. Only 6 out of 10 teenagers take an orthodox,

Christian view of God, defining Him as "the all-powerful, all-knowing, perfect Creator of the universe who rules the world today." Four out of 10 teens maintain a different view of God. One out of five hold a "New Age" outlook. To them, either everyone is God, or God is a word meant to infer the total realization of personal human potential, or there are many different gods, or "god" merely refers to a state of higher consciousness that a person may reach. And for many teenagers, the search for God is still in progress: one out of five do not know what God means or how to define God.

A majority of teens (55 percent) believe that when people of different faiths pray to their respective gods, they are really all praying to the same central power source. They grant that each faith group may use different names for their supreme being and may communicate in different ways. But in the end, there is one core force that represents the characteristics we attribute to God. Most teens do not seem overly troubled about the lack of definition of those attributes.

To a growing number of teens, the name (or description) "God" is an elastic expression: it can be stretched to cover just about anything you want it to imply. When teens talk about God, they may be alluding to a unique and holy being, a genteel universal spirit or an amorphous and impersonal higher power.

The implications of this a-deification of God are serious for those who wish to promote a biblical version of the Christian faith. We are told in Scripture to possess a fear of God, to be in awe of Him, to acknowledge His power and holiness, to accept His love and to serve Him. The subversion of the identity of God has rendered many of these responses impossible among our teens.

Fear of God? Frankly, our research suggests that teenagers have a greater fear of walking the streets of their neighborhoods or wandering the hallways of their schools after hours than they have of God.

Stand in awe of the Creator? Again, we find that the practical nature of millions of teenagers renders them more likely to stand in awe of the natural talents of Michael Jordan, the physical strength and grace of Shaquille O'Neal, the dexterity of Eddie Van Halen, and the physical beauty of Cindy Crawford or Claudia Schiffer than to bow down to the immeasurable capacity of God.

The holiness of God? Holiness is an oblique concept to the high schoolers of today. In fact, a surprisingly large percentage of teens believe that God Himself sinned!

Accept God's love? Most teens are not sure what this means. How do you embrace the love of an impersonal, invisible, removed spirit? Can you trust a being who created (or seemingly idly allows) war, hatred, disease, hunger and pain to give genuine love? In a culture where skepticism supersedes trust and the need for tangible proof has replaced confidence in people's claims, teenagers seek evidence that God loves them. Once it is abundantly clear, perhaps then they will accept it.

Serve God? Ever the tangible and pragmatic group, teenagers are likely to view serving people as a more appropriate behavior. Don't misunderstand me—there is absolutely nothing wrong with serving the homeless, the poor, the infirm or others who are disadvantaged; Christians are called to do these very things. But the motivation for good works must be considered. Naturally, a motivation other than seeking to serve God and reflect His love to a hurting world does not negate the positive influence of those works; but neither does a non-Christian motivation serve to glorify God. Among most teens, their desire to create a better world through occasional service to humanity is far removed from their spiritual perceptions and inclinations.

THE AFTERLIFE

Among teenagers, there is a tremendous amount of intrigue—and shockingly limited concern—about life after death. Although most of these young people have at one time or another been exposed to the Christian view of salvation, most do not embrace that theology.

One of the most significant discoveries from our research among all age groups of the population has been that most people make their lifelong, faith-shaping choices when they are young. If a person is ever going to become a Christian, the chances are great that he or she will do so before reaching the age of 18. About three-quarters of all people who have consciously, intentionally and personally chosen to embrace Jesus Christ as their Savior did so before their 18th birthday.

This realization is of no small consequence. Churches spend the vast majority of their evangelistic dollars (more than 70 percent of it, by some of our preliminary research) on trying to penetrate the adult market. After decades and decades of such toil, we can confidently announce the results: such efforts bear little fruit. On the other hand, the amount of money and effort we pour into reaching kids with the gospel pays off relatively handsomely. This fact demands that we ask why we don't concentrate evangelistic efforts on youth.

Currently, we find that almost 6 out of 10 teens claim they have made a "personal commitment to Jesus Christ that is still important in their life today." However, the confusing rhetoric and worldly snares that kids address is evident in the fact that only about 6 out of 10 of those young people believe that they will live eternally with God because they have confessed their sins and have accepted Christ as their Savior. Amazingly, one out of four teens who says he or she has made a personal commitment to Jesus believes in living eternally for reasons other than God's grace granted through Christ's death and resurrection. Most of those individuals are relying upon their own good behavior or laudable efforts. The remaining youths who have made a commitment to Christ generally say they have no clue what will happen to them after they depart from this planet.

TABLE 6.1
SPIRITUAL PERSPECTIVES, BY GENERATION

Statement About Their Faith	Teens	Adults	Busters	Boomers	Builders	Seniors
Have made a personal commitment to Jesus Christ that is still important in their life today.	57%	65%	61%	68%	72%	70%
Believe that when they die, they will go to heaven because they have confessed their sins and have accepted Jesus Christ as their Savior.	33	39	34	39	48	34
God is the all-powerful, all-knowing perfect Creator of the universe who rules the world today.	60	70	70	70	70	68

For a large number of Americans, the key time of decision in life is in the 10- to 12-year age span. Although kids in this age range constitute only 4 percent of the population, it is the time frame when more than one-quarter of all believers decide to follow Jesus Christ. Of course, it is likely that much educating and preparation went into bringing these young people to such a point of decision. But it is helpful to recognize that not only do many people make their life-changing decisions before they even reach high school, but also that such a compressed time period has such major consequences.

In fact, if we stretch the age frame to 8 through 13 years of age, that six-year stretch of time defines when roughly half of all Americans made their decisions to become true Christians. In other words, by the time students enter high school, the odds of accepting Christ as Savior are radically reduced; by the time they graduate from high school the odds are stacked against such a choice to a staggering degree.

Many Paths

The research we have conducted among teenagers also shows that large numbers of them do not believe that Jesus Christ is the only means to eternal peace. There is a growing trend toward universalism among America's young people. In the spirit of cultural diversity, more and more teens are allowing that all religious faiths have value, offer equally valid solutions and ought to be given a fair hearing before they make a choice.

The foundation for this open-mindedness among teenagers is their stand on moral truth. By an overwhelming margin, teens reject the notion of absolute moral truth in favor of a relative view of right and wrong. Three-quarters of all teens say there is no such thing as absolute moral truth; 4 out of 5 teens argue that nobody can ever be absolutely positive that they possess the truth of a situation; 9 out of 10 young people assert that what is right for one person may be wrong for someone else in exactly the same situation. More than 4 out of 10 teens go as far as to claim that you can tell if something is morally or ethically right "if it works."

From a spiritual point of view, the all-roads-lead-to-heaven mind-set is widely ingrained. Half of all teenagers state unapologetically that it doesn't matter what faith you embrace since they all teach similar lessons. And millions of teens espouse the philosophy that it doesn't really matter what you believe, it's what you do that counts. Two out of every three (67 percent) believe that "if a person is good enough, or does enough good things for others during their life, they will earn a place in heaven." Half of them say that all good people, whether or not they consider Jesus Christ to be their Savior, will live in heaven after they die.

As a general rule, modern teenagers reject any individual, organization or philosophy that claims to be the sole proprietor of goodness. Our culture defends diversity at all costs and demands respect for all viewpoints, no matter how wacky or pernicious. These same encompassing views apply to the spiritual outlook of teens. Even many of those who are committed Christians bristle at preachers and other church leaders who promote the Christian faith by playing it off against the validity or legitimacy of other faith traditions. To quote the multibillion-dollar New Age fairy tale of the '90s, *The Lion*

King, we are all just part of "the circle of life"—the unending connectedness of humanity that is eternally present and must live in harmony.

GOD VERSUS THE CHURCH

There may have been a time in American history when people held a two-part desire: to be close to God and to be active and productive participants in a local church. If that combination did exist, it has surely been frittered away with the passage of time.

These days, teenagers struggle to identify the value of a church. They do not view churches as productive, insightful or comforting. They rarely find churches to be places that dispense wisdom, provide constructive development, facilitate meaningful relationships or provide public service. They view churches as antiquated organizations designed to promulgate "religious stuff" and to "live apart from the world instead of getting involved in the pain of the world."

To their credit, teenagers are more focused on God than on the institutional church. Almost 6 out of 10 of them say they want to be close to God; not quite 4 out of 10 say they are anxious to be active participants in a church. Developing a close, personal relationship with God is of deep interest to most of them because they really want to be connected to something more significant than themselves. Until they find that "ultimate significant other," they will rely largely upon their own abilities and instincts to get them through the daily challenges. But they're on the lookout for legitimate spirituality.

ON THE BIBLE

The vast majority of teenagers own Bibles. As we will see in the following chapter, though, the primary functions of the Bible are to serve as a bookend, a symbol of religiosity or as a sign that they are indeed "Christian."

Although they do not use it much, an amazingly large proportion of teenagers argue that the Bible contains useful and valid information. For instance, we discovered that among the kids who label themselves "Christian," 6 out of 10 maintain that the Bible is "totally accurate in all of its teachings." As a reliable source of guidance for an emerging generation, the Bible represents an underutilized tool to which kids have access but that is often overlooked in their search for answers.

In fact, we learned that most teenagers actually defend the Bible. When posed with the negative view that "the Bible does not provide practical standards for living in today's world"—a statement that makes sense culturally—only one out of every four teenagers agreed. Further, three out of four teens agreed that "the Bible provides a clear and totally accurate description of moral truth."

Now that seems to contradict their view that there is no such thing as absolute moral truth. Upon deeper exploration, however, it turns out not to be contradictory at all. Teenagers believe that the Bible is one of many sources of truth. And because no person can tell another person that his or her truth is inadequate or invalid, the Bible provides truth for some people and not for others—just as the Koran, the Torah, the I Ching or the *Wall Street Journal* are sources of moral truth and meaning for others.

BEHAVIOR AND FAITH

Most teenagers acknowledge that faith ideally should influence their lifestyles.

Defining Sin

Sin is a difficult concept for teenagers to comprehend. Most of them believe that the notion of sin is still pertinent to our age—only one out of every six teens (16 percent) argue that "the whole idea of sin is outdated." The problem is not in accepting that there can be sin, but in determining what is sinful and what isn't. After all, if there is no absolute truth defining sin is quite elusive: what may be sin for you many not be sin for me At least the fundamental acceptance of the concept of sin still lives on in the lives of tomorrow's leaders.

Another positive reality is that 6 out of 10 teens concur that God has established limitations on human behavior and that actions that conflict with those limits lead to negative consequences. Again, the challenge comes when it is time to determine what those limitations are, and whether or not the consequences of transcending the limits are severe enough to restrict our behavior.

Clearly, there is errant thinking aplenty on the sin issue. Consider these striking revelations. First, nearly half of all teens (45 percent) contend that "when Jesus Christ was on earth, He committed sins, just like other human beings." Second, one-fourth of the teen population believe that some sins or crimes are so serious that even God cannot forgive them.

Invasion of Privacy

Both of these contentions—that Christ sinned and that some sins cannot be forgiven—serve as clear indicators that a lot of questionable theology is weighing down America's young people.[1] Lacking much exposure to the Bible itself, and coming from a generation that relies more heavily on emotionalism than empiricism for guidance, the opportunities for heresy are prolific.

Reflect on the implications of the pair of counterfeit contentions just described. These views are currently embraced by literally millions of teens and appear to have a significant degree of influence on the thinking and behavior of many young people. In fact, I invite you to eavesdrop on the ruminations of a hypothetical but typical teen as he or she reflects upon spiritual truth and redemption.

> Okay, so Jesus committed sins. Well, then, He's clearly not much of a Savior, is He? He's certainly not the pure and holy God many claim He is. And if He committed sins, chances are He won't be much of an advocate for my worthiness to get to heaven. That pretty much eliminates the value of Christianity and all that church stuff.
>
> But wait a minute. Maybe, because He sinned, sinning is okay. Maybe the issue is your intentions, not your actions. Heck, everybody makes mistakes—even Jesus. After all, Jesus is allegedly in heaven and is loved by God the Father, so maybe the issue isn't purity after all, but just trying to do your best.
>
> But then again, there is no such thing as absolute moral truth. That kinda knocks the very notion of sin out of the equation. There can't be such a thing as sin if there is no consistent, absolute standard to define sin—unless, of course, I chose to define something as sin. If I tried to tell someone else they're committing a sin, though, that'd demand a belief in absolutes, and I don't buy that. And if I am the only one who can define sin, why would I define any of my own actions as sin? My intentions were good, just inadequately thought through.
>
> And if there's no sin, well, who needs a Savior? There's nothing to be saved from. I try hard, I do nice things for other people, I even do some religious things sometimes, like praying, going to church, giving money to poor people. If I don't need a Savior, then what's all this fuss about Jesus Christ and salvation and the forgiveness of sins? I guess the best course of action is

to be good, try my hardest, and not worry myself sick about stuff that isn't so deep or scary after all.

Add to these mental gymnastics some other entrenched elements of bad theology accepted by a majority—namely, that there is no such thing as Satan or an evil force, and that the main purpose of life is simply enjoyment and personal fulfillment—and we have the makings of a generation that is prone to reflect on the finer matters of Christian theology without understanding the basic foundations.

It all brings back to mind the observation of the late Allan Bloom, the college professor who authored the best-selling exposé of our culture a decade ago, *The Closing of the American Mind* (Touchstone Books): "Today's students no longer have any image of a perfect soul, and hence do not long to have one. Yet they have powerful images of what a perfect body is and pursue it incessantly."

We all establish our goals and priorities according to the core values and beliefs we cherish. Based on what we can discern about the core values and beliefs of today's teenagers, we have ample reason to be concerned about the plight of the nation.

Note

1. There is, of course, the possibility that teens might be thinking of "blaspheming the Holy Spirit," for which there is no forgiveness. It is doubtful, however, that many teens have even heard of this, much less incorporated such a consideration into their theology and practice.

7 MAKING FAITH REAL

As a relational generation, many aspects of teenagers' lives are more attractive or meaningful when done in a group setting. Behaviors as diverse as dating and exploring the Bible are more enjoyable or take on a deeper significance for many teenagers when done in the company of peers. In much the same way that the most brutal punishment for highly extroverted children may be to send them to their rooms, so isolation from peers causes a sense of loss among most teenagers.

This desire to experience and explore life as part of a group of trusted, like-minded peers extends to their religious discovery process as well. Although most teenagers have no sense of church history or much comprehension of the true spiritual purposes of the Church as a united body of believers, they do relate to the shared experience that church-based activities allow.

So there is some good news regarding teenagers and the Church. First, many teens are spiritually inclined, and therefore are open to giving the local church at which they find themselves a chance to prove its worth. This means that teenagers are not making decisions about future church involvement without experiencing firsthand what the church is like. The vast majority of teenagers have had prolonged periods of time during which they have been involved in the life of a Christian church. In fact, even as the massive spiritual assessment process goes on, the evidence points out that most teens are somehow connected to a Christian body of believers today.

But the bad news is that many teenagers, having been exposed to and been participants in the teaching, worship, study, prayer and other central activities of the Christian Church, are already making their getaway plans. They have given the Church a fair shot at convincing them to stay. Their exposure to the Church in action, however, has led millions of them to choose to end their interaction with institutional Christianity once they have the freedom to do so.

You Could See It Coming

Put into proper context, this is not terribly surprising. Teenagers have always had a penchant for rejecting the activities older Americans revere. In fact, teenagers have traditionally used their transition from high school to adulthood (e.g., college, jobs, marriage) as a natural breaking point from their childhood activities. The desire to stop going to church is one of the time-honored traditions of that transition.

But just as importantly, teenagers are maturing in an environment of rejection. Adults are not only consenting to the act of rejecting traditional or reasonable conditions, they are taking the art of rejection to new heights. Pick up a newspaper or news magazine and read about the nation's temperament. Americans are in a rejection mode these days. The culture of the '90s has been described in very vivid language by social analysts: the culture of disbelief, the sour society, a nation of victims, the culture of complaint and the picky people. No matter what we receive, it seems that it's never right—and we react with a vengeance.

Teenagers cannot help but see the trail of temper tantrums we throw. We divorce the people we used to love and whom we promised to stick by no matter what. Blacks and whites are still at each other's throats, and Hispanics are now a part of the battle. We give new television programs two or three weeks to prove themselves before we yank the plug—and the plug is pulled in most cases. We deny a majority of the immigration applications submitted. We throw incumbents out of office. Eight out of ten new businesses go belly up within five years. Nine out of 10 new products never make it. Our nation's relationships with foreign countries are constantly renegotiated and reevaluated, resulting in longtime relationships souring and new partnerships taking the forefront. The typical direct mail sales campaign is deemed successful if it is turned down by "only" 98 percent of the people who receive the mailing. The public schools are losing ground in favor of private schools and even home schooling. You name it, we don't like it.

The process of rejection has invaded the religious scene, too. Adults have been departing from religious involvement and rejecting longstanding religious practices and products at a steady clip for some time now. Perhaps it began a few decades ago when they started to reject the mainline Protestant denominations, then denominations altogether. Then it was the *King James Version* of the Bible, replaced by an unending stream of new versions, translations and paraphrases.

Next to fall into disgrace were traditional styles of worship, followed down the tubes by some time-honored traditions (e.g., women cannot be ministers, churches must have Sunday evening services, preachers should wear robes, etc.). Every year introduces more rejections of what was formerly sacred: some of the changes are reasonable, some are change for the sake of change, but the bottom line is that rejection of the past is becoming de rigueur.

So why shouldn't teenagers question and then reject the Church? Although young Americans have been devoted to an aggressive search for truth, purpose, meaning and authentic spirituality, so have their parents—and, after all, haven't their parents pretty much decided to turn their backs on the Church?

THE CHURCH LIVES ON

Given this context, then, the truly remarkable circumstance is that teenagers have any relationship with Christianity and with the local church, and that they have any degree of personal spiritual pursuit still intact. The presence of such a relationship in this environment of rejection and dissatisfaction is testimony to teens' spiritual resilience and innate need for deeper and more spiritual meaning.

In fact, the research we have conducted among teens reveals that they are unusually well connected to churches. Indisputably, the Christian Church in America is ailing, but that condition is not attributable to a widespread rejection by teenagers. In some respects, the Church retains a greater measure of potential and hope for the future because of the dogged spirituality of teenagers.

Consider the current levels of religious participation among teens.

Half of all kids attend a church worship service each week. As might be expected, the older teenagers become, the less frequently they attend church services, declining from two-thirds of all 13-year-olds attending church each weekend to less than half of all 18-year-olds. The most astounding realization in this regard is that teenagers are more likely to attend a church service every week than are adults.

Two out of three kids pray during the week. Three out of four pray at least once a month.

One out of three teenagers reads the Bible during a typical week, and half of these will read it at least once a month. Encouragingly, the data point out that kids in the eleventh and twelfth grades are actually more likely to read the Bible during the week than are younger kids. In fact, juniors and seniors in high school are more likely to read the Bible each week than the typical adult in the United States.

One out of every three teenagers participates in a Christian youth group in a typical week. Half of all kids 13 to 18 years of age have some involvement with such groups at least once a month. Not all of these groups are sponsored by a church, however; a large number of kids engage in spiritual activities through a parachurch ministry such as Youth for Christ, Young Life, Student Venture/Campus Crusade for Christ, Fellowship of Christian Athletes, Son Life and literally hundreds of other independent, transdenominational entities.

One out of every four teenagers takes part in a Bible study group of some sort. Often, these groups appeal to teens because of the relational opportunities, more than the Bible discovery component.

Almost 4 out of 10 teens show up at a Sunday School or Catechism class each week. This involvement drops precipitously as the youngster ages, from 63 percent attendance among 13-year-olds down to just half that level among 16- and 17-year-olds.

These are amazingly high levels of religious activity—at least in comparison to those of adults. Granted, many of these young people attend religious activities under pressure from their parents, but the fact remains that most teenagers engage in some form of corporate religious activity during the week.

ALL OR NOTHING

One of the most intriguing findings from our research is the pattern of frequency with which kids get involved in religious activities. If teens get involved in such an activity—whether it is a worship service, a midweek youth group, or a Bible study group—the chances are very high that they will be there every week until they drop out. Relatively few teens who attend any type of religious activity do so just once a month or less frequently. Either they're into it, or they're not.

This is consistent with the behavior of this generation. These teens are usually quite intense about the endeavors in which they participate. They are totally into it or totally separated from it. That's not to say that teens don't benefit from some adult coaxing. Regular contact with the leaders of the group in which they're involved helps to maintain the longevity of teens' commitment to the group. Nevertheless, when teens get involved in something, if their initial experiences suggest that the activity is meaningful and provides value, they are likely to be regular until they decide that particular activity does not have value or provide personal benefit.

CHRIST MADE THE SCHEDULE

Another surprising reality is how few teenagers who describe themselves as Christian have calendars that are unencumbered by religious activities. Just 1 out of every 10 teenagers who is at least nominally Christian never attends a church service, Sunday School or Catechism class. Only 5 percent of the nation's teenagers who say they are Christian do not pray. Even some of the more taxing, less common activities are part of the lives of most teens: Only 1 out of 5 never reads the Bible, and just 3 out of 10 never attend a church-based youth group. The least common religious activity among those we tested is being part of a Bible study group.

To put this into context, recognize that the religious activity levels of teenagers is higher than that of adults for every activity we evaluated. There are, however, two noteworthy differences between adults and teenagers when it comes to religiosity. First, the involvement of many teens in religious endeavors is part of their spiritual exploration process. Millions of them are seeking a sufficient degree of experiences and information to enable them to determine whether Christianity has a role in their future. Thus, there may come a time in the near future when their involvement in faith activities will come to a screeching halt. In contrast, most adults who participate in corporate Christianity have already decided that the Christian faith is the most appropriate faith system for them and that regular involvement in faith activities is justifiable. Sometimes adults reevaluate their lives and reduce their spiritual activities, but that is much less likely than is true for teenagers.

Second, a substantial number of teens who take part in religious activities do so upon the insistence of their parents. The motivations of parents are multifold: it reflects the parents' personal fulfillment from faith endeavors, their perception that religious training prepares a child for life, the belief that kids who are exposed to religious principles become more virtuous individuals, and the declining but still existent perception that a good parent is one who instills a religious perspective in their children. In contrast, adults who participate in Christian activities have no such authority figure compelling them to do so; their involvement is strictly voluntary.

And don't lose sight of a fact described in the previous chapter: a majority of teenagers who are involved in spiritual activities take part in those adventures along with family members. The research is quite clear: the more involved the family is in religious activities done together, the more likely the teenager is to engage in religious activity, to expect to continue those religious pursuits upon leaving home, and to perceive religion to be significant and additive in life.

Talk It Over

But teens do not take part in religious opportunities solely because of family pressure. For many of them, spirituality is a central part of their lives. Their involvement reflects who they are at their core. Millions of teenagers could no sooner envision their lives without a spiritual component than they could imagine their lives without friends, food or fun times. In millions of situations, parental prodding to engage in religious rituals is simply part of the push-pull process that makes parent-child relationships so unique. If the parents had not begged the children to participate, many of them would have carried out the behavior on their own, simply because they feel driven to explore faith.

For instance, a majority of teenagers (59 percent) believe they have a personal responsibility to share their religious beliefs with other people. That is an extraordinarily high proportion of young people who see themselves as evangelists for their particular set of religious views. In fact, to place it in context, this is about double the proportion of adults who feel this same compulsion.

Isn't it ironic that at the same time Congress and the adult population are battling about protecting kids in our schools from exposure to overtly Christian thought (called, in politically correct lingo, subjective religious influence), the kids are embroiled in some rather frequent and intensive interactions among themselves regarding that very subject matter? Our research shows that the debates about school prayer, Bible reading in the schools, extracurricular religious clubs and religious instruction in schools is an artifact of baby boomer struggles with issues such as control and ideology. Boomers become offended bv public efforts at proselytizing. Teenagers enjoy the interaction. Few of them make a big stink about the religious cleansing issues that so occupy the minds of many parents.

Religion is part of this generation. In fact, two out of three teenagers have discussed their religious beliefs with their peers during the past three months. Debates regarding religious beliefs are common among teenagers. Among some segments of the teen population, at least three out of every four teens engage in such verbalized reflections on faith matters. Kids from the South, "A" students, conservatives and teens whose families are religious are among those who are most likely to talk regularly with peers about spirituality.

Social pressure to discuss spiritual matters has affected many teens, too. Among those who contend that they have personal responsibilities to share their religious perspectives with others, one-third have not even had a discussion with their friends about spiritual matters during the past three months. This raises another reality about teens: when they are forced or expected to do something, and they either do not understand the reasons or do not feel a sense of ownership of the expected behavior, they simply will not engage in the behavior.

CHURCH REPORT CARD

Most teenagers have had regular involvement with a church. As we evaluated their perceptions of the performance of churches, however, we discovered that churches are better at facilitating some outcomes than others.

Slightly more than 4 out of every 10 teenagers (43 percent) who describe themselves as Christian said that churches do an excellent job of making them more caring and concerned for other people. Forty-four percent said churches help them make decisions about what is right and wrong, and the same proportion said the church helps them understand what they believe spiritually.

Somewhat fewer teens—slightly more than one out of every three—said they have found that their churches have done excellent jobs in helping them understand themselves better (34 percent); helping them apply what they believe to their daily lives (36 percent); providing them with a greater sense of purpose for their lives (38 percent); helping them maintain or develop meaningful relationships with their peers (36 percent).

Among the outcomes we tested, the activity at which teens believe churches are least adept is helping them relate better to their parents. Only one out of every four said his or her church has done an excellent job in this regard.

Overall, the reactions of teenagers to what their church has done indicates that churches are most competent at helping young people question and rethink some of their perspectives about people and lifestyles. The churches seem less helpful when it comes to putting those perspectives into practice. Unfortunately, this is an area in which no individuals or institutions—parents, teachers, church leaders, or other authority figures—perform with consistent excellence. It is also one of the most important areas—the place where "the rubber meets the road."

The significance of so few teenagers citing their church as providing excellence in its ministry is that teens, like all Americans these days, expect excellence. Teens invest what they perceive to be a lot of resources to take part in a church's ministry: their time, their reputations, their energy and their spiritual focus. The fact that not a single outcome was evaluated for which at least half of the teenage Christians awarded their churches top rating is the precursor to their departures. They cannot be faulted for not giving the Christian Church a try. Some church leaders may complain that teens' expectations or standards are too lofty and therefore unattainable. But teen standards are what they are. The bottom line is that for the majority of teenagers who have given the Church an opportunity to minister to them, the Church simply did not measure up.

FUTURE PLANS

So what would you anticipate is going to happen with most teenagers? Will they stay or will they leave the Church? We have seen that they are living in an atmosphere of rejection; they are inclined to seek spiritual truth through a process of relational and unintentional exploration; they have given the Christian Church a chance to prove itself and emerge indifferent to those efforts; and yet they remain more active than other Americans in their spiritual quests.

It should not be surprising that most teens admit that the chances of their leaving the Church are at least as good as the chances of staying. Only two out of every five teens (41 percent) said they are "very likely" to attend a church once they leave home. Roughly as many (36 percent) said they may attend, and the remaining one-quarter (22 percent) said the chances are slim to none. These figures have to be taken with a grain of salt because people are notoriously poor at predicting their future behavior, especially when they have little sense of what their personal circumstances will be. In the case of teenagers, most have only the vaguest notion of what life will be like for them a year or more down the line, after they have left home for an undefined place and purpose. In fact, two decades of research has shown us that people usually overestimate how likely they are to engage in a particular activity. If that pattern holds true for teens, that is bad news indeed for the development of the organized Church in the United States.

This is a subtle evaluation of the churches that teens attend. They will vote with their feet once they reach 18, or whenever they are given the lifestyle freedom to determine their own spiritual choices.

The kids most likely to remain in the fold are those whose lives are most likely to resonate with the theology and the lifestyle expectations of evangelical Christianity. The teen segments who were most likely to predict their continued involvement with the Church included "A" students (53 percent said they are very likely to remain churched), girls, students living in the South, teens whose sociopolitical views are conservative and those currently connected with a Protestant church.

Also of great significance is the fact that kids whose families are very involved in spiritual matters are almost eight times more likely than kids whose families have little or no religious involvement to say that they will continue to attend a church even after they leave home.

REPULSIVE RELIGION

Let me offer three thoughts on other reasons we may find many of today's religiously involved teenagers dropping out of church life within the next 5 to 10 years.

The perception of inflexibility. We have noted that as teenagers age, they have a greater tendency to use their brains. The older they get, the less accepting they are of rules and imposed truths. I'm not saying that the Church should not stand for anything, but merely making the observation that when an individual or organization stands firm on emotionally charged issues or takes too many inflexible stands that demand strict adherence, many teenagers bolt.

In churches across America, my observation has been that many reach teens by using signals that the church is user friendly (e.g., rock music; fast-paced, energetic games and activities; overt friendliness). They impress teens by developing forums that allow for the delivery of information in ways that are creative and intriguing. But then they lose teens because the bottom line is delivered in such a heavy-handed manner that kids feel used, manipulated, programmed and unheard.

This is a generation that requires the ability to start its evaluation of Christianity by denying or rejecting its principles before entering into a sincere consideration of those truths. This group studies something not by reading and memorizing, but through debate and searching for examples of the principle in real life. Many of these teens never get that far in the process, because they feel that those who profess to define Christianity are too closed-minded to allow for an honest debate and examination of the guts of Christianity.

The sense of many teens is that after the games and good times have ended, and the real discovery process is initiated, the defenders of the Christian faith take a "this is it, take it or leave it" attitude, prohibiting the necessary verbal jousting. Consequently, they contend that they are given insufficient latitude to subject the Christian faith to deep and intense scrutiny. Disallowing such a serious challenge is their clue that Christianity is not the meaty, resilient faith it had been cracked up to be. Sensing that the line has been drawn in the sand, they simply turn around and move in a different direction, seeking new spiritual horizons to examine.

No room in the Church. A second key is to recognize that many teenagers will leave the Church because they will feel that the Church encourages them to do so. Apart from the disappointments many will experience when they are not permitted to tear the faith apart before trying to put it back together and own it as their own, millions of kids will graduate from high school and never be pursued again by a church until later in their adult years.

Our research shows that the most spiritually vulnerable time for a person is between the ages of 18 and 25. A wealth of life transitions are occurring during that period of time. Most of them have a balanced tension: push from one end, pull from the other. Not so when it comes to their church lives, though. Most people in this age bracket will leave home and never be seriously pursued by a church until they are settled and with child.

This does not perturb most young adults because they are beginning to experience freedom, responsibility and decision-making options like they have never encountered before. Few of them will feel guilty about abandoning the Church; they will feel abandoned by the Church—unless they return, at which time they will find that they are the in-between group with whom nobody knows how to deal.

Think about it. From cradle to graduation, they have been focused upon and programmed to death within the Church. But what happens at age 18? They are too old for high school ministry, but too young for the young adult ministry. Amazingly few churches have a college-age ministry group, and the majority of those in existence are small, plateaued and placid. The message transmitted to these "tweeners" is that the Church doesn't have a place for them. They adapt accordingly—by participating in other endeavors.

Different wavelengths. A third reason many kids may leave the Church is because they process information differently from how we assume they do. As we develop our youth ministries and attempt to unfold the timeless truths of Christianity for our presumably eager learners, what we take to be sympathetic ears may be something quite different. We believe they need to understand Christianity, and we teach accordingly. Many of them believe their need is to understand spirituality, people and faith, so they filter the teachings they receive differently from what we expect. In other words, we share the same physical space, but we are operating on different mental and emotional wavelengths. Our goals are not the same. No matter how superbly we communicate about Christianity, much of our information may be received in an entirely different way from what we even imagined to be possible.

It Ain't Over Till It's Over

But if our efforts to gain and retain the teen segment of America have not been completely successful, all hope is not lost. We can expect that millions of teenagers will continue their spiritual journey and explore other faith groups. We might anticipate that many teenagers will simply excuse themselves from organized religion for a few years. That doesn't mean they will give up the chase, but simply that it will take a different form and they will travel down different roads.

But the power of God's Word, the depth of His compassion and the impact of His truth and principles should never be underestimated. We can certainly reshape our ministry efforts in light of what we have discovered about today's teenagers to minister more effectively and to enhance the possibilities of their deciding that Christianity is the appropriate spiritual path to pursue.

To fail to upgrade our efforts when we know they can be improved is a sad commentary on our desire to serve God with all of the excellence we can muster.[1] At the very least, we must always seek to understand those whom we wish to reach with God's truths, so that we may not be yet another obstacle the Holy Spirit must overcome in the eternal battle for the souls of teenagers.

But we should not become discouraged by the fact that their spiritual paths are dissimilar from our own, or that they deviate from our expectations. It is a competitive spiritual marketplace in which we minister, and we must expect people to sample what we have to offer and then to give other faiths—or no faith—the same opportunity to prove their worth. Fortunately for us, we serve the only true God, the only powerful deity in existence, and a Creator who loves these kids so much that He will not cease to pursue their hearts. In their own unique way, they are a challenge to us to persuade them to follow James's admonition: "Come near to God and he will come near to you."[2] For unauthentic faith is unconvincing if not hypocritical. To a seeker, our faith will ring true or hollow depending on its authenticity.

Notes

1. This principle is clearly defined in Colossians 3:23.
2. James 4:8.

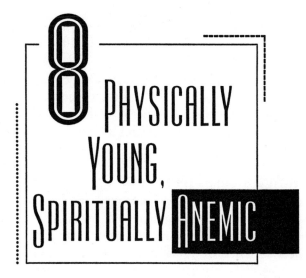

8 PHYSICALLY YOUNG, SPIRITUALLY ANEMIC

Thankfully, one-third of the teenage population have beliefs that characterize them as born-again Christians. God is alive and at work in the lives of millions of teenagers!

But while the Boss is doing His part, we must wonder if we are doing ours in nurturing teenagers who trust Christ for their salvation. During this survey, seeing how teenage believers deal with life was consistently startling. It did not take much of an imagination to wonder sometimes if the Christian faith of these young people really makes any difference at all in how they think about, perceive and handle life.

I am grateful for the enormous effort poured into youth ministry by the thousands of Christian youth workers across the nation—but simply getting teens into a youth group is not enough. I am pleased to find that millions of teens attend a worship service on a weekly basis—but being in the sanctuary at the appointed time is not enough. How wonderful that the majority of teens own or have easy access to a Bible, and that more than 5 million teenagers read it every week—but exposure to the Bible does not take matters as far as they can go.

Forgive me for a chapter if I seem overly harsh or critical; I hope my frustration is expressed constructively, not destructively. I truly am appreciative of people's prayers, efforts and commitment of financial resources to reach and influence young people. I simply feel that we are not hitting the mark. Bear with me as I describe the basis of my concern about how we are nurturing and challenging the young people who have chosen Christ as their Savior.

Evaluating Teenage Claims

There are two ways to evaluate the attitudes and behaviors of teenagers who have accepted Christ as their Savior. First, we can compare them with teenagers who are not disciples of Christ to see if there is a discernible difference. Second, we can compare the Christian teens to an absolute standard. Let's do both.

Are Born-Again Teens Different?

When we look at how the born-again kids think and live in comparison to their non-Christian peers, there are some encouraging signs and some not so encouraging signs. Among the not-so-encouraging signs is the fact that the behaviors we tested are virtually identical among Christian and non-Christian teenagers. Both segments were equally likely to volunteer their

TABLE 8.1
The Behavioral Differences Between the "Saved" and the "Lost" Are Minimal

Perspective	Born Again	Not Born Again
Discussed your religious views with other kids your age?	79%	56%
Ever felt like you were experiencing God's presence?	64	33
Volunteered your time to help needy people?	49	44
Ever watched an X-rated or pornographic movie?	32	41
Cheated on a test, exam or other evaluation?	29	27
Had sexual intercourse?	23	29
Stolen money or some other material thing?	6	7
Looked through a pornographic magazine?	5	8
Used an illegal, nonprescription drug?	4	11
Tried to commit suicide?	3	7

TABLE 8.2
Born-Again Teenagers Have More Traditional Views About Family and Marriage

Perspective	Born Again	Not Born Again
God intended marriage to last a lifetime........97%		79%
If the traditional family falls apart, American society will collapse. 57		42
These days it's almost impossible to have a successful marriage. 26		28
Anyone who gets married these days should expect their marriage to end in divorce. 6		12
It would be very desirable to have one marriage partner for life. 89		76

time to help the needy, to cheat on an exam, to steal possessions, to look through a pornographic magazine, to have had sexual intercourse, to have attempted suicide and to spend time watching MTV during the week.

Born-again teenagers were slightly less likely to have watched an X-rated or pornographic movie or to have used an illegal, nonprescription drug within the last three months. They were also more likely to have discussed their religious beliefs with other kids their age and to have felt God's presence at some time in their lives. Overall, however, apart from their engagement in religious activity, most teenagers' lives do not seem to have been substantially altered by their faith views.

Among the encouraging signs, however, is that born-again kids hold views on marriage and family that are more in line with biblical mores than do non-Christian youth. They are more likely to perceive that God intended marriage to last a lifetime; more likely to uphold the importance of the traditional family to the health of our society; and less likely to believe that divorce is inevitable for people who get married.

Teenage believers are also more likely to assert that having just one marriage partner for life is a very desirable circumstance. Overall, the differences between the views of the Christian and non-Christian teenagers on family issues are not huge, but at least the nature of the existing differences are as we might hope for: the Christian teens are more likely to have a biblical position.

TABLE 8.3
THE DREAMS OF BORN-AGAIN TEENS ARE SOMEWHAT DIFFERENT FROM THOSE OF THEIR NONBELIEVING PEERS
(% DESCRIBING THESE PERSPECTIVES AS "VERY DESIRABLE")

Perspective	Born Again	Not Born Again
Having a clear purpose for living.	86%	75%
Having a close relationship with God.	83	45
Being personally active in a church.	65	23
Influencing other people's lives.	63	48
Making a difference in the world.	61	48

TABLE 8.4
LIFESTYLE VIEWS DIFFER

Perspective	Born Again	Not Born Again
God established limits for humankind; acting in conflict with those laws has negative consequences	74%	55
The main purpose of life is enjoyment and personal fulfillment	49	71
Lying is sometimes necessary	45	63
One person cannot really make much of a difference in this world	8	22

When it comes to their desires for the future, born-again youths clearly have a greater desire to live a life that is both spiritual and purposeful. The believers were comparatively more interested in having a close relationship with God, having a clear purpose for living, influencing other people's lives, making a difference in the world and being active in a church. Interestingly, the biggest margins of difference related to the spiritual perspectives: The born-again kids were much more desirous of being close to God and active in a church. The believers were only somewhat more likely to want to make a difference, have influence and live with purpose.

Attitudes about the meaning and conduct of life are also notably distinctive for born-again teenagers. The believers are more likely to believe that conflicting with the limits and laws God set for humankind will result in negative consequences, and are less likely to state that the purpose of life is personal fulfillment and enjoyment, or that one person cannot make a difference or that lying is sometimes necessary.

TABLE 8.5

PERSPECTIVES ON TRUTH DIFFER

Perspective	Born Again	Not Born Again
What is right for one person in a given situation might not be right for another person in a similar situation.	92%	90%
When it comes to matters of morals and ethics, truth means different things to different people; no one can be absolutely positive that they know the truth.	66	87
There is no such thing as absolute truth; two people could define truth in conflicting ways and both could still be correct.	59	78
You know that something is morally or ethically right if it works.	33	47

Perspectives on truth are revealing. We found that the Christian teenagers were more likely than their non-Christian counterparts to believe that absolute truth exists, and less likely to contend that no one can know if they possess aspects of truth. They were also less likely to believe that something must be ethically or morally correct if it works. They are indistinguishable from their peers when it comes to believing that right and wrong in a given situation differ from person to person.

Believers also assume very different views of Scripture from their nonbelieving counterparts. Teens who have accepted Christ as their Savior are more likely than other young people to contend that the Bible describes moral truth, and that it is accurate in everything it teaches. They are less likely to state that the Bible fails to provide clear standards for living, and that reliance upon it for moral guidance is foolish.

There are also significant distinctions between believers and nonbeliev-
ers when it comes to their respective views on faith matters. Born-again
teens are more likely to argue that the Christian faith is relevant these days,
and that they have a personal responsibility to share their religious views
with other people.

Christian teens are less likely than their nonbelieving peers, however, to
suggest that Satan is merely a symbol of evil; that salvation can or must be
earned rather than accepted; that Jesus committed sins during His earthly
ministry; that all religions teach the same lessons and pray to the same God;
that some sins are too serious to be forgiven; and that the very concept of
sin is antiquated. The believers are also much less likely to adopt a New
Age view of God.

TABLE 8.6

TEENS WHO BELIEVE IN JESUS ARE ALSO MORE LIKELY TO BELIEVE IN THE BIBLE

Perspective	Born Again	Not Born Again
The Bible provides a clear and totally accurate description of moral truth.	91%	62%
The Bible is totally accurate in all of its teachings.	85	46
The Bible does not provide practical standards for living in today's world.	14	33
Anyone who relies upon religious faith or the Bible for moral guidance is foolish.	6	12

So what does all of this mean? First, we can thank God that the teenagers
who are striving to follow Him seem to have been influenced in a positive
direction toward affirming His values and adopting lifestyles that would be
more pleasing to Him. No reasonable human being would argue that it is
difficult to be a teenager these days. And no one should challenge the
courage of teenage Christians who are striving to buck the trends of their
generation to think, believe and act differently as a result of their faith.

Granted, we do not know if these young people live differently because
they accepted Christ, or if they accepted Christ because they were inclined
to live differently and found Christianity to be a faith system that corre-

sponds with their internal perspectives and inclinations. The bottom line, however, is that they are different in measurable ways from their peers. Indisputably, God will honor that (and so should we). Standing up for Jesus Christ and the ideals He represents is neither popular nor easy as we close out the second millennium.

TABLE 8.7

CHRISTIAN TEENS HAVE A DIFFERENT VIEW OF SPIRITUAL MATTERS FROM THEIR NON-CHRISTIAN PEERS

Perspective	Born Again	Not Born Again
The Christian faith is relevant to the way you live today.	93%	76%
You, personally, have a responsibility to tell other people about your religious beliefs.	82	45
If people are generally good, or do enough good things for others during their lifetimes, they will earn a place in heaven.	43	83
The devil, or Satan, is not a living being but is a symbol of evil.	42	66
Muslims, Buddhists, Christians, Jews and all other people pray to the same God, even though they use different names for their God.	36	69
When He lived on earth, Jesus Christ was human and committed sins, just like other people.	31	55
It does not matter what religious faith you follow because all faiths teach similar lessons.	30	64
All good people, whether or not they consider Jesus Christ to be their Savior, will live in heaven after they die.	27	61
Some sins or crimes are so serious that they cannot be forgiven by God.	14	27
The whole idea of "sin" is outdated.	8	22

Compared to an Absolute Standard

Second, we must consider that in terms of absolute standards—trials and tribulations notwithstanding—the attitudes and lifestyles of teenage believers have a long way to go to satisfy the biblical standards set for us. Perhaps, as many have said, Christianity is not so much a destination as a journey; expecting everyone to have reached the end of the road and to uphold every biblical admonition to perfection is unreasonable. We are, after all, human beings—tainted by a sinful nature, living in a world of temptations, snares and distractions. And when we're talking about teenage believers, we're focusing upon people who have not been Christian very long. They have had just a few years, in most cases, to understand their faith and to set about transforming their lifestyles and thinking patterns to correspond with the ways of Christ. Teenagers, perhaps even more than most, are a work in progress.

Yet, it is important for those of us who wish to enable and empower teenagers to become all they can be in their relationship with Christ to recognize some of the pitfalls and traps they may encounter, if they have not done so already. As we endeavor to instruct, mentor and model Christianity for them, we must know enough about who they are to focus on the things that matter and to emphasize elements that require special attention.

When we evaluate the lifestyles, attitudes and beliefs of Christian teens in comparison to a biblical standard, the picture is not encouraging. What we find is a segment of young people who have turned their hearts over to Jesus Christ, but who are struggling to connect their faith with daily reality. As examples, among our Christian teens we find the following conditions:

- Six out of 10 say there is no such thing as absolute truth.
- Nine out of 10 say that right and wrong depend on the individual and the situation—that is, they espouse moral relativism.
- One out of four deny the notion that acting in disobedience to God's laws brings about negative consequences.
- One-half believe that the main purpose of life is enjoyment and personal fulfillment.
- Almost half contend that sometimes lying is necessary.
- One out of three say that as long as something works, you can be sure that it is morally or ethically right.
- More than 4 out of 10 say that Satan is just a symbol of evil, not a living force.

- One out of three Christian teens contend that Jesus Christ committed sins while on earth.
- Three out of 10 say that all faiths teach the same lessons.
- About half of the Christian teens in America maintain that people can earn their way into heaven through good works or exemplary behavior.

TABLE 8.8

CHRISTIAN ADULTS AND CHRISTIAN TEENS HAVE VERY SIMILAR VIEWS

Perspective	Teens	Adults
The Christian faith is relevant to the way you live today.	93%	92%
You, personally, have a responsibility to tell other people about your religious beliefs.	82	76
If people are generally good, or do enough good things for others during their lifetime, they will earn a place in heaven.	43	32
The devil, or Satan, is not a living being but is a symbol of evil.	42	46
Muslims, Buddhists, Christians, Jews and all other people pray to the same God, even though they use different names for their God.	36	48
When He lived on earth, Jesus Christ was human and committed sins, just like other people.	31	27
It does not matter what religious faith you follow because all faiths teach similar lessons.	30	43
All good people, whether or not they consider Jesus Christ to be their Savior, will live in heaven after they die.	27	29
Some sins or crimes are so serious that they cannot be forgiven by God	14	27
The whole idea of "sin" is outdated	8	11

LIKE TEACHER, LIKE STUDENT

My intention is not to condemn or even scold our teens for having views that conflict with the teachings of the Bible. In fact, my major concern is with the adults who teach kids about Christianity.

Troubled by the theological perspectives among Christian teens, I went back to our data from surveys among adults. My investigation showed that there is a very close parallel between what Christian teenagers believe and what American adults believe. It doesn't take a rocket scientist to figure out what the real problem is in this situation. Just take a look at the items for which we have parallel information between Christian teens and adults.

The information shows an unusually close parallel between the younger and older Christians. And we thought they weren't paying any attention! If anything, the information suggests that we may have taught today's teens too well the same things we, as the "mature" Christians, believe. The real problem is that many of us believe errant doctrine.

The information also points out that there is one overall difference between Christian young people and Christian adults: young people are more likely to be accepting of all people; they are "more comfortable with diversity of expressions of faith" and "less quick to judge other people."

This tension between judgment and discernment is evident in all parts of the Christian Church today. It is one of the great points of division between conservatives and liberals, between mainliners and evangelicals. More so than the older generations, the teenagers within the body of believers tend to assume that good people, or people who have tried their best, will earn God's favor. They are less territorial about the rights to God's kingdom.

Clearly, a problem is plaguing young people today. Although millions of them want to follow Jesus and are doing their best to follow the advice and example provided by the Christians who are guiding their spiritual development, they have a problem with the reliability of their mentors. When the disciplers provide spiritual noise rather than a means of discerning the true voice and calling of God, the Church is in dire straits.

9 NEW RULES, NEW CHALLENGES

Circus acrobats have it easy compared to teenagers; at least the acrobats run through their paces with a safety net. Teenagers these days are living on the edge, constantly at risk in various dimensions of life. The safety net that used to protect them from imminent disaster has eroded. They used to have stay-at-home mothers, two-parent families, small classroom sizes with attentive teachers, a bevy of community service organizations that looked out for their best interests and personal development, a neighborhood of familiar and caring faces, adequate police protection and churches to which they felt connected. Today, the net is frayed.

But teenagers are a hearty breed and have simply responded by adapting as best they can to their deteriorating environment. They are increasingly independent and self-reliant, taking care of business in the most effective way they know how: by themselves.

NEW RULES

The adaptation process has ushered in a new and continually evolving set of rules. The old assumptions about how teens think, how they see people and circumstances, and how they will respond to their view of reality are no longer valid. Although the new rules that teenagers accept make many adults uncomfortable, the new paradigm is rational and logical, given the rapid and transformational changes that have capsized our culture since 1980.

Most of the new rules reflect the best effort teenagers can muster at coping with new cultural realities. The vantage point on which the rules are based unveils the growing pains of teens. Their rules simultaneously reflect naïveté and street smarts; compassion and disdain; vulnerability and protectiveness; fear and courage. These unique responses to their unique reality are neither viewed as nor intended to be new; they are simply the most reasonable reaction teens are able to provide in response to a bewildering and overpowering adult world.

The discomfort adults feel with these new rules is merely a reaction to the fact that a determined, large and independent generation is embracing a different worldview and set of goals than that of adults. Teenagers, on the whole, are dismissing the values, standards and goals of the older population without apology or apparent agonizing. This is a blow both to the individual egos and the collective spirit of the boomers, in particular. It also means that older people have to work harder not only to understand teenagers, but also to exert significant influence upon their activities. One of the greatest challenges to people in positions of authority is to understand the new rules and to work strategically to maximize the positive effects and minimize the negative possibilities associated with these shifts.

Here are some of the evolving new rules that define and direct teenagers in the mid-1990s.

New Rule #1:
Personal relationships count. Institutions don't.

Organizations that have played a major role in the shaping of America this century hold limited promise of maintaining their influence in the coming decades. Churches, prestigious universities, government, major corporations, the courts—all are invested with authority by the majority of the population, but their positions as influence agents are tenuous among teenagers. Whether there is enough zeal and persuasiveness left in the prevailing system of institutions and power relationships to motivate the young to accept and respect these institutions remains to be seen.

In the interim, the elements that will define purpose, value and direction are personal relationships and interpersonal networks. Teens, as is true of the buster generation overall, are much more dependent upon personal relationships as a barometer of health and welfare than are boomers and builders. Teenagers are less likely to worry about the impact of philosophies and dictates on the society as a whole than they are to consider and protect the needs of the individuals they know and care about on a personal level. The teen population usually opts for that which is most tangible. "Society" is not an easy concept to grasp.

New Rule #2:
The process is more important than the product.

Teenagers are typically more enthusiastic about participating in a decision-making process than they are in passively accepting the outcomes of that process—even if the results of that process are totally consistent with their needs or desires. Again, this is contrary to the modus operandi of prior generations, for whom the ends justified the means. For teenagers, the means are at least as important as the ends. This is partially because they believe they have been demeaned if they do not have a say in the determination of their reality, and partially because they wholeheartedly believe that their participation will both enhance the process and improve the results.

A common attribute of teenagers throughout the past few decades has been their strong distaste for monolithic power centers or hierarchical systems. Today's teenagers are taking that distrust and disrespect for authority and position to new heights. Because they do not accept the basic values of the dominant generations, they have less fear, trepidation or conscience about disobeying the majority. They do not see their denial of adult commands and procedures as rejection; rather, it is simply their fulfillment of their responsibility to be true to themselves and their future. Their obstinateness is more than a statement; it is a necessary behavior.

New Rule #3:
Aggressively pursue diversity among people.

The acceptance of cultural diversity by young people is more than just a tip of the hat to the politically correct movement. As teenagers (and other busters) examine the world they will someday inherit, they see much that disgusts them. One such element is the American thirst for homogeneity. Such sameness is usually imposed and can be individually stifling. Whereas boomers might think of homogeneity as a means of minimizing disruptions and irregularities, or of reducing the unpredictability of life, teenagers view the move toward homogenizing society as cultural neutering.

Teenagers are at the heart of a generation that has witnessed tremendous degrees of cultural diversity: the "browning" of our population; the splintering of the media to allow for a broad array of tastes and preferences in music, reading interests and televised entertainment; entrepreneurial and decentralized businesses; technological breakthroughs that have restructured interpersonal communications and relationships toward making them more evenhanded; and truly integrated neighborhoods in which people of all economic and ethnic walks of life have the ability to live in physical proximity to the types of people who formerly were removed from their world.

For many older Americans, such diversification of our culture is unnerving and threatening. For teenagers, sociocultural diversity is both normal and desirable.

New Rule #4:
Enjoying people and life opportunities is more important than productivity, profitability or achievement.

Teenagers have yet to enter the marketplace or to take on full-time family responsibilities. Taxes are not yet a burden for them and they are only minimally concerned with global economics and politics. For the most part, their lives are sheltered from the intricacies and pressures of corporate profit levels, consumer spending trends and the national debt. Outpacing Japan and Germany are matters that seem to concern their parents but have no moorings in the world perspective of teenagers.

Overall, kids in the 13 to 18 age range have adopted a more basic goal for their lives: to know others and to be known by them. Theirs is an existence that revolves around the heart rather than the mind. This may change as they move through the life cycle, adding more and deeper responsibilities to their agenda. But today, teens see people at the heart of the goals they have established for themselves, rather than as obstacles to reaching a more materialistic or power-driven set of goals.

New Rule #5: Change is good.

The typical adult struggles with change: the process, the necessity, the practice and the personal implications. Teenagers, though, have grown up in a world that has been radically reinventing itself every decade. Change is barely perceptible to them; only its absence would seem abnormal. Adults fume and fulminate about the constant shifting that reshapes our daily reality. Teenagers enjoy the unpredictability and the constant change of scenery.

If the world were to slow down and minimize the degree of innovation and structural transformation, teenagers would feel cheated out of the joy of experiencing the new and creative, the novel and mysterious. Theirs is a future filled with turbulence; but it is turbulence only to outsiders who look in and, having lived in tranquility, have a different context for interpretation. Teenagers may not have a clear vision of the future they are striving to create, but that is partly because the portrait of that future is always changing. And they would have it no other way.

New Rule #6:
The development of character is more
crucial than achievement.

Amazingly, teenagers are more likely to have a biblical perspective on the human condition (i.e., it's who you are that's important, not what you do) even though they are only nominally familiar with biblical principles or content and rarely read the Bible. In fact, though they possess this outlook, they would not assert that it is drawn from the Bible. It just so happens that their natural inclinations and the principles of Scripture coincide in this case.

Teenagers are only nominally motivated to achieve overt dominance and to gain public adulation for personal achievements. They are more interested in enjoying life (which, to them, does not correspond to professional ascension or prominence) and being the type of person who can add to (and enjoy) a sustainable future existence. They may not study as hard or pursue professional activities as steadfastly because they are driven by the heart rather than the head.

New Rule #7:
You can't always count on your family to be there for
you, but it is your best hope for emotional support.

Kids these days still view their families as the best and most reliable support mechanisms available. However, they have experienced enough divorces (within their own family or those of friends and relatives), have witnessed sufficient personal disappointments at the hands of family, and have such skepticism about social systems and traditional lifestyle patterns that they have conceived a protective shell that says their families may not always be there for them.

Thus, although most teens believe they can usually count on their families to be loving and helpful, they consider the possibility that at some point they may find themselves all alone. This dangling fear colors their perspective on family, friends and personal behavior. Count on them to hold back some of their loyalty, vulnerability and accessibility, just to be on the safe side. Teenagers do not want to be burned by inappropriate family decisions or behaviors.

New Rule #8:
Each individual must assume responsibility for his
or her own world.

To the average teen, allowing the prevailing social systems to allocate resources on their behalf invites disaster. Being a kid no longer means enjoying a few more years of relative ease and burden-free exploration. Now it means accepting responsibility for the development of the world in which they live as soon as they have that ability. Such responsibility embraces a wide range of realities: sexuality, faith, personal finances, grooming, compassion and social activism, environmental sensitivity, ethnic justice and so forth.

The concept of youth has been stripped of its Pollyanna innocence. Their experiences in the urban jungle has caused them to be mature beyond their years, stressed beyond what's reasonable. They may bleed their emotional heartaches by whining about unfair conditions, and drown their disappointments in desperate attempts at finding sympathy and support, but their conclusion is simple: Look out for yourself because no one else will.

New Rule #9:
Whenever necessary, gain control—and use it wisely.

Baby boomers are the living example of what happens when control is the central objective of life. Teenagers recognize the importance of control—and the temptations, tragedies and responsibilities that accompany it. They are reluctant to chase such weighty responsibilities at the same time that they are weary of being trampled by those who possess and abuse control. The only alternative is to judiciously assert themselves to control that which is in their best interests—not control for its own sake, but control as a means to a reasonable end.

Unlike the boomers, who have grabbed control because it was available and because it is a means to ascending the power ladders of society, teenagers and their older buster kin opt for power and authority as a means to a superior society, a living environment that is in concert with their values and perspectives. They are not jealous when others have power, as much as they are fearful of abuses resulting from selfishness and a skewed view of humanity, globalism and spirituality.

New Rule #10:
Don't waste time searching for absolutes. There are none.

Teenagers are not as obsessive about time as boomers have proven to be. They do realize, however, that there is more to experience in life than time allows for, so time is a precious resource to be carefully spent. One of the avenues teenagers are not likely to pursue, without coaxing and good reason, is a spiritual or philosophical quest for absolutes. They see no payoff at the end of the process, largely because their observation has been that people who perceive moral absolutes to exist live no differently and do not seem to have more attractive values or keener influence than do others.

From the teenager's vantage point, the process of identifying moral absolutes seems incapable of enhancing life in tangible ways. Further, teenagers have no burning moral need to identify absolutes; given their assumption that all morality and ethics is relative, why search for anything different? To teens, the best strategy is to accept the fact that there are no moral absolutes, and to live with it.

New Rule #11:
One person can make a difference in the world—but not much.

One of the shaping perspectives of teenagers today is that they have to learn to be content with a smidgen of progress because that may be all they can generate. Teens are wary of the boomeresque view that one person can change the world. Given their congregational mentality, teens are more likely to see the value of connecting with a group of like-minded people who, together, can have a synergistic influence on their corner of the world. They are setting their standards lower than the boomers did—but they see this not as a downsizing but as a rightsizing of vision. They contend that lowering the bar is their way of being realistic and sane about what can and cannot be done.

Teens are leery of falling prey to emotional stress, burnout, disappointment, anomie, severe depression and social humiliation. They do not want to sacrifice their friends and family for personal crusades that ultimately leave them empty and morose. In the end, they may make some of the same blunders as their predecessors, but they will not make them out of a denial of the possible consequences of their falsely heroic actions.

New Rule #12:
Life is hard and then we die; but because it's the only life we've got, we may as well endure it, enhance it and enjoy it as best we can.

Teenagers seem to have a pretty down-to-earth view of reality. They never really had a chance to experience the naive enthusiasm and idealism that motivated preceding teen populations. They are not as passionate or driven as their predecessors. In fact, they are alarmingly objective about life.

On the one hand, this takes some of the spontaneity and the exuberance of discovery out of daily experience. On the other hand, teens may have a healthier understanding of themselves, their world and their future, and may therefore prepare for and cope with life on their own terms and with less agitation than adults suffered when they were teenagers.

In fact, assuming that their lives will be less satisfying than prior generations have experienced or expected also serves to heighten the potential for surprisingly positive outcomes. In other words, if you set the standards low enough, then surpass those standards, the exhilaration level may sky-rocket in response to the apparent overachievement.

And if you're wondering why the teenage work ethic is so hard to find, it's because their elders never focused on passing on the legacy of hard work; and teens themselves have other goals in mind.

New Rule #13: Spiritual truth may take many forms.

There may be one mighty and perfect God, there may be none, or there may be many. Today's teens are more comfortable with multiple alternatives in every walk of life—including spirituality—because they do not buy the assumption that important realities are black or white. Whether their friends embrace different gods or no God is insignificant to them because they are neither worried about nor offended by the spiritual choices of others.

To teens, religious pluralism is sacred; imposing any religious beliefs upon another person is the only universal sin. In fact, for millions of teenagers, faith is not so much a matter of discovering the truth as it is a matter of identifying and expressing a personal preference in a dimension of life that offers opportunities for freedom and emotional safety.

Aggressive evangelism offends most teens. They are not offended by a person's religious beliefs, only with someone's insistence that they are right and that others must conform to their lead. Teenagers believe that it is more important to have a faith system that works for the individual than for the individual to agonize about finding the "right" faith system and striving to convert the masses to that system.

New Rule #14: Express your rage.

Teenagers harbor loads of anger and rage toward society, based on their experiences of broken families, corrupt politics, a ruined natural environment, a bankrupt global economy, the absence of authentic relationships and values, spiritual confusion and manipulation, and a sense of generational abandonment by the prevailing powers of the culture. Consequently, teenagers' responses have been irritating to older people—responses such as expressing unfiltered rage (rap music, politically correct rhetoric), massive law-breaking events (spring-break seizures of beach and desert communities), anger and profanity demonstrated publicly (on-line services, tabloid TV programs) and commonly raised sentiments identifying themselves as victims of a callous, immoral and visionless society.

To teens, they are the underclass, the population niche with nothing to lose and nothing to hide. Why contain the rage that has built up inside and is so justifiable? Although they may reflect antipathy toward getting ahead in light of traditional standards, they find outlets for their pent-up frustrations and discouragement and believe that the failure to vent their hostilities would be yet another injustice.

New Rule #15: Technology is our natural ally.

Every generation develops its own styles of communication and its own language. The teenagers of today are part of a generation that has not truly created a musical sound that is unique; their custom-made language is that of the technological world. While most adults are still confounded about how to program the clock on their VCRs, the average teenager is at home creating new applications on their personal computers. As boomers tinker with conventional software applications, teens are surfing the Internet in search of the outrageous. Cutting-edge technology to a boomer is a CD player; to the teen, a CD-ROM is a must.

As they look to the future, teens see technology as one of the few unspoiled territories they may yet utilize to build a viable future. Where older people see technology as a tool to be harnessed, teens view technology as a means of expression to be unleashed. In the battle for supremacy and authenticity, technology may prove to be the secret weapon of teenagers and their generation.

NEW ERA, NEW RESPONSES

One of the tough truths of ministry is that it takes place within a culture. We aren't called to love the culture, only to recognize, understand and deal with it. As we consider the new rules by which teens will live their lives for the next half decade or more, we have to realize that we are not called to sit back and pompously pass judgment on the rules they have created and pursued, but to acknowledge the reality they are creating and to address the reality that these rules exist and have influence in their lives.

Each generation has a unique set of rules by which it lives. The introduction of these rules by teens in the late '90s is disturbing to most ministry leaders and concerned adults because they signal an end to the rules we had just gotten used to, and because these new guidelines may conflict dramatically with the rules to which our own generations conform. If we are serious about connecting with and influencing teens, though, getting a grip on their rules is a crucial step toward knowing them and having the opportunity to challenge and support them in their maturing process.

Remember, we don't have to appreciate the rules, only the people seeking to live by them.

10 AND TEENS THINK *THEY'RE* UNDER STRESS

Every age group has circumstances they dread. School-age kids live in fear of the pop quiz in school or having to visit doting Aunt Wilma. Teenagers fear a breakout of zits, being called on in class when they don't know the answers (but the kids they want to impress are watching), having to explain unexpected low grades on their report cards, being caught by the principal and failing the driver's test at the Department of Motor Vehicles.

For parents, the fear is much easier to identify: that their little boys and girls will someday turn into teenagers.

The march of time is unstoppable. Sooner or later all of us who have kids will face the Death Valley days of parenthood ushered in by our little ones' 13th birthdays. But there are ways we can make the most of the teen years. The research informs us of a few steps and strategies we might take to minimize the pain and maximize the joy of living with the monsters we have created.

Youth workers can also take some steps to get the most out of their experience with our young people. Youth workers have a different set of motivations for their involvement in the lives of teens. They have different expectations and responsibilities in their relationships with teenagers. But youth ministers also undergo a tremendous time of testing at the hands of teens—a process that can result in both joys and frustrations. Because youth workers have the ability to work with kids and then leave them—a luxury parents sometimes wish they had, but that by definition (if not by law) is not on their menu of choices—circumstances must be developed that permit them to have positive involvement and influence.

CHALLENGES TO ALL WHO DEAL WITH TEENS

Whether you are a parent, youth worker, youth pastor, high school teacher or someone else who works with teens, a few common threads of behavior and thought will help the young people with whom you interact.

Effective influencers of teens are those who remain abreast of current trends and conditions related to the teen world. Understanding the fears, the opportunities, the dangers and the worldview of teens helps an influencer to comprehend teenagers and to respond strategically. We do not have to buy into everything they say, do or promote, but we must know and understand those realities.

A Philosophy of Where You're Going

The most effective influencers also have a predetermined philosophy of life and a philosophy of youth influence. In other words, the most effective parents are those who know where the boundaries are, what the possibilities may be and what they are seeking to achieve (or allow to be achieved) in the lives of their youngsters.

Nonparent influencers typically have a similar mental framework that enables them to make good and consistent decisions regarding the activities and perspectives of teens. Waiting until a predictable situation occurs to determine how to handle that circumstance often results in bad decisions that are the products of confusion, anger or emotional shock. Anticipating potential situations and thinking through how to deal with them ahead of time allows for more rational, creative and effective responses.

The most effective means of influence is to adopt a firm but interactive style. Teenagers, especially in the late '90s, resent and resist imposed standards. They are often not opposed to the standards as much as they are resentful of how those standards were presented and instituted. The influencers who make the biggest dent in the thinking and lifestyles of teens are those who enable them to understand and own the parameters they need. Discussing the problems, potential solutions and preventative courses of action can enable teens to believe they have a stake in both the proceedings and the outcomes. It is that sense of participation that makes the standards more palatable and more likely to be implemented.

But leaders who are not accessible to teens are unlikely to have much influence on them. Credibility comes from involvement; involvement requires availability. Teenagers whose parents spend little time with them also have shockingly little impact upon the thinking and behavior of their own teenagers. We have found that adults who wish to influence kids must be open to being with those kids. Accessibility not only permits modeling and interaction but also conveys a sense of compassion and caring. Teens do not want to feel managed as much as they need to feel cared for. Availability is one of the clues they examine to ascertain if they are simply being "handled" or if they are being nurtured.

Answering to God and Others

The influence agents in teen lives have a responsibility not only to the teens, but to God, the Church and society, too. Adults who work with teenagers are obliged to model the principles they pass along to kids. And they are equally obliged to ensure that the theological base of those principles is sound. At some point, we may have to answer to society for how we indoctrinated and equipped our young people. We may be absolutely certain that some day each of us will answer to God for the influence we had upon each young life. Influencing young people is not a responsibility to be taken lightly.

This is also a reminder that we must pray consistently for teenagers. If we care about them, then we undoubtedly recognize the pressures and challenges they face. Often, they are ill-equipped to handle those temptations and snares alone. We may not be physically present with them at all times, but we can certainly provide for them a spiritual covering through prayer. To fail to pray for our teens is to reflect a lack of concern about their development and safety.

A final challenge that all teen influencers have in common is the need to provide practical assistance for them in addressing the difficulties and opportunities of life. Whether we are teaching the Bible, discussing family issues, reviewing homework assignments or considering relational options they face, we must provide tangible assistance to young people. It is one thing to speak and behave in such a way as to shape their values, attitudes and beliefs. It is quite another challenge to help them cope with the immediate needs of their lives.

Youth leaders have the privilege of enabling and empowering teens to do what is right, what is best and what is necessary. We must acknowledge that the privilege comes with responsibility and demonstrate our worthiness through the depth and excellence of our investment in the practical needs of our teenagers. We must help them by teaching them mundane matters such as how to open a bank account to more sophisticated routines such as how to use the personal computers they have at home. At times, they may seem too remote or too mature to require (or benefit from) such help. Most of the time, though, they desire real help.

A Personal Challenge to Parents

Parents have additional responsibilities and opportunities that are unique to parents. Let me touch on just a few.

After conducting a variety of studies among teenagers in the past decade, teaching in a public high school and serving as a leader in a church's high school ministry, two critical views I would like to impress upon the parents of teenagers are: *Do not get divorced,* and *make time for your kids.*

Of course, parents must do many things to maximize their positive influence and to satisfy their obligations as parents. But unless a teen's parents are willing to maintain a true family environment and to sacrifice their time for the benefit of their kids, the effects of the rest of their parental behaviors and perspectives will be severely blunted.

Not long ago, as I was compiling research data in preparation for writing *The Future of the American Family,* I was astounded at the research regarding the importance of an intact family. The mass media and the entertainment industry certainly have not read the same research—or, if they have, they have chosen to ignore the facts. The importance of the family environment upon the character, the emotions and the worldview of a young person—and ultimately upon adults—would be hard to overstate.

Going Against the Grain

When I talk about the importance of maintaining a unified family, it is not without an understanding of the magnitude of this expectation. We live in a society that expects and accepts divorce. Almost 3 out of every 10 marriages in America end in divorce (although not the 50 percent the media commonly claim). Significantly, the prevailing attitude among adults—7 out of 10—is that if the marriage is struggling, the decision of whether to stay together or separate should not be influenced by the presence or needs of the children in that family.[1] More than one-third of married adults have affairs. Millions admit that if they could do it all over again, they'd marry someone else. No, I am under no illusions that marriage is a simple and automatically fulfilling partnership.

But sometimes the truth is hard to hear. The Bible is quite clear in its teaching about God's intentions for marriage and family. Further, God's instructions to us about family contours have been clearly and unarguably verified in recent sociological research. Stated in its simplest form, when the parents divorce, their kids suffer. Although divorce has some profound and disturbing effects upon the adults involved in the separation, the dissolution of the family has its most devastating effect upon the children. Kids who live with a single parent or in a blended family struggle with issues that are nonexistent in the lives of kids raised in an intact family.

The kinds of issues with which young people struggle, from a behavioral and attitudinal vantage point, include satisfaction with life, self-image, friendships, hopes for the future, trust in people, belief in God, academic achievement and interest in helping others. Research by psychologists has concluded that many other issues affect kids of divorced parents not only during their childhood and adolescent years, but also during the remainder of their lives.[2] God intended families to be unified, permanent units. Our decision to tamper with His design has serious and long-term consequences that are evident and measurable.

I am not so naive as to believe that divorce can always be avoided. In some instances, such as situations in which one parent physically or sexually abuses the spouse or children, divorce may be necessary to protect the children from harm. The statistics about divorce, however, show that such instances represent the minority of cases. Most often, parents divorce because they get tired of each other and refuse to work on overcoming their differences or to invest time and energy in their relationship. They succumb to the pressures, stresses and trials of daily life—and sometimes to the sexual and relational temptations offered by alternative lifestyles and opportunities.

Counterbiblical Americans

The notion that we may abandon our family responsibilities when we get tired of our pressures and stresses, however, is one of the most clear-cut examples of the selfishness and irresponsibility of modern Americans. And it is decidedly counterbiblical. Imagine God modeling such an attitude for us. Envision God hearing the prayer of Jesus from the garden of Gethsemane in which His beloved Son asked for a way out of the coming humiliation and suffering if it was within the Father's will. Had God been an American in the late '90s, He would have recalled the many occasions on which the Pharisees and Sadducees had given Jesus a hard time. He would have anticipated the betrayal by Judas. He would have considered the hardened hearts of the religious leaders and the worldly perspectives of the Romans. He would have been exasperated by the ignorance of the apostles, most of whom still had no clue regarding Jesus' life and ministry. In the end, God would have tossed in the towel and spared Jesus from the cross—and we would have suffered eternal separation from Him as a result. That would be the ultimate divorce.

But God was true to His human family and provided an escape route through the suffering Servant. He made good on His promise to honor us as we honor Him. He chose to do what was best for those whom He loved and to whom He had obligated Himself.

The teen years are perhaps as difficult a time as any parent will experience in his or her life. So often the kids whom parents have so diligently raised for more than a decade suddenly become uncontrollable, unrecognizable monsters. The persecution of parents at the hands of teenagers creates a host of relational pressures and antagonisms between husbands and wives. For many spouses, a time comes when any escape route looks better than continuing to experience the pain and failure that parenting a teenager catalyzes. But the decision to divide the family will bear long-term negative dividends for the parents, the teens, their siblings and society at large.

Strategies for the Battle

So if you are the parent of a teenager (or may become one in the near future), how can you endure one of the toughest challenges you may ever face in your life? Here are some ideas passed along by parents who have been there and seem to have emerged embattled but victorious.

Surround yourself with a team of peers who can advise and console you. Having an outlet for your concerns and frustrations is useful. Hearing what other parents of teens are going through helps you realize you're not a lousy parent; it's just a predictable stage kids go through. Getting good ideas and perspectives from someone who can empathize gives strength and hope. Don't be a lone ranger of a parent. Lean on other parents for strength.

Resolve that divorce is simply not an option, and that you and your spouse are committed to God, to His Word, to each other and to your kids. When things get tough, get in the habit of discussing the issues with each other and striving to work it out. Unless you make such a recommitment to your faith and family, the chances of your standing tough in the face of severe pressures challenging your marriage and home life are slim. Make that commitment today—and renew it openly and regularly.

Seek the help of an objective, seasoned, trained third party to help clarify issues, facilitate communication or provide a useful overview of the situation. That outsider may be a pastor, family member, counselor, elder or someone else who can provide unbiased, caring and biblical insight into your situation.

Work with your spouse to create opportunities to be together (e.g., scheduling dates, doing special activities without the kids). Take advantage of those opportunities to talk through issues. Communication is key.

Pray alone and together (if possible) that God will heal whatever rifts have splintered your marriage.

Search out mature mentors. Invite another couple from your church whose relationship seems biblically grounded and emotionally functional, and who recently had kids the same age as yours, to serve as peer mentors. Go out to dinners or desserts with them and talk about the mechanics of how to handle the stresses of marriage and of raising teens. These mentors may not have the exact answers you need, but their wisdom and experience may guide you to more appropriate decisions than you might have made otherwise. Just hearing that others have gone through similar struggles and have come out of the process alive might be enough to enable you to persevere.

If you and your spouse dissolve your marriage, the chances are overwhelming that your teens will suffer. It is difficult to model godliness and strength for them when you abandon a family member and the promises you once made to that partner. In a marriage breakup, it's more than just the adults who launch a new life. Unfortunately, most kids do not have the maturity and the emotional tools to handle such a new beginning positively. If one of your goals in life is to provide the nurturing environment and resources to allow your kids to succeed in life, providing a home with a male and female adult influence is an irreplaceable step toward that end.

THINKING PARENTING THROUGH

As parents, we're forced pretty early in the game to develop some semblance of a philosophy of parenting. For most people, that mind-set is not clearly articulated; it is more of a subconscious series of impressions and expectations that are integrated into spontaneous decision making regarding our interaction with teens.

Gearing Up for a New Phase

Parents of teenagers often state that it seems everything they've done in the past as parents seems incredibly irrelevant once a child hits age 13 or 14. Teens bring new meaning to words such as emotional turmoil, rebellion, conflict, stubbornness and challenge. Parents who have lived through the teen years warn their peers that coping successfully with the challenges of raising a teen demands that parents perceive their tasks as new phases of parenting. Each prior phase—infancy, preschool, kindergarten, elementary school and adolescence—introduced new challenges and permitted parents to fairly gracefully make the transition into a more sophisticated parenting role.

But the onslaught of the teen years is a rude and abrupt transition in which the loving, energetic and predictable child who has lived under the same roof with you for a dozen years can suddenly become your worst nightmare. The only way to successfully work through the teen years is to reevaluate the parenting philosophy that enabled you to make it through the early years, and update it to address the realities of handling teens and the new kinds of pressures they feel and exert upon the family.

It seems that the parents who are most effective at guiding and empowering teenagers are those who have planned ahead in how to deal with likely situations. This allows parents to either anticipate problems and take preventative action (e.g., working through concerns about sexual involvement before the teen becomes sexually active) or to take remedial steps swiftly and thoughtfully after an episode occurs, rather than reacting out of emotional paralysis, anger or confusion. The issues that teens' parents face are predictable and identifiable; those situations may be unique for the family, but they are rarely unique to the teen world. How you handle those behaviors and situations relates to your parenting philosophy, your parenting style and the nature of your relationship as a family.

Character—Not Just Behavior

It has proved useful for many parents of teens to identify character traits they wish their youngsters to embody. Focusing upon character, rather than strictly upon behavior, is one way of precluding a constant repetition of undesirable behaviors. Developing that kind of character should, of course, start when the child is young; many experts would say that if the process has not been underway for many years before the child reaches the teen plateau, then it is too late to effect much change in the youngster's character. The need for shaping and refining character, however, is applicable at any age.

Philosophically, teens' parents must also determine what kind of balance they wish to achieve between discipline and positive reinforcement. Both elements are necessary, although "balance" does not infer an equal emphasis on both inputs. In talking with teens, their concern was that their parents do not provide enough positive affirmation. In speaking with parents, their concern was that they had not adequately disciplined their kids. The ideal balance is probably somewhere in between.

Creating the Right Environment

Part of the issue is the environment in which teens grow up. For instance, many parents bemoan the grip that television holds on their kids. Yet they do little to curb their appetite for the tube or to monitor and limit the kinds of programs their kids watch. Effective parents tend to limit the amount of viewing time, prescribe the programs that are suitable for viewing and provide attractive alternatives to TV for their teens.

Effective parenting also means developing a seamless integration of spirituality and daily activity. The teenagers who fared best in life—academically, relationally, attitudinally, spiritually and behaviorally—were those whose families had regular times together for prayer, Bible reading, church attendance and discussions about faith, values and morality. It is ludicrous to assume that families that do not emphasize the spiritual dimension will develop children who decide to embrace religion as a major, positive shaping force. One of the greatest legacies parents can leave their children is an intense and significant sense of God's presence in their lives. It won't happen on the high school campus or from watching prime-time TV. It may happen if the parents decide that introducing spiritual truth is a primary parental function.

Having said this, however, I would be remiss if I did not also underscore the fact that the teen years are extremely difficult for teenagers. They need boundaries, but they also need some space—that is, some latitude that will enable them to explore, experiment, fail and mature through their own abilities and filters. Parents need to be ready with the safety net and to guard the boundaries they have set up as limits upon teen life. But smothering teens with restrictions that are too tight may not serve them any better than the absence of boundaries. Finding the balance between limits and freedom is one of the elements that make parenting an art—and one of the demands upon parents that nobody else can accomplish as intelligently and strategically.

Hands-on Parenting

Although teens give the impression that they want total independence, they realize that at times they need a helping hand—even if it comes from their parents. But how can a parent know where to draw the line about what is desirable and appropriate and what is deemed meddling and irritating? Truly, the distinction depends upon the nature of the relationship between the parent and the teenager. Our research, however, suggests that the assistance parents can most safely render to their teens includes the following:

- Helping them with their homework;
- Teaching them conflict resolution;
- Discussing emotional disappointments;
- Discussing fears they face, such as death and rejection;
- Discussing values.

Notice that the verb "discussing" was used to identify the useful input that parents might provide to kids. The verb was not "imposing"; attempts at mandating certain views or beliefs will generally fail. We have been sending these young people to school for years, training them how to think and rewarding them for those times when they think most clearly. For them to grow up and be in a position where they need to think for themselves, and then to disallow them from doing so, brings on tremendous frustration, disillusionment and distrust.

Building the Relationship

The bottom line when it comes to parenting is the ability to develop a deep and loving relationship with the teenager. Of course, this is easier said than done. How can such a relationship of trust and mutual enjoyment be developed?

Parents of teens have divulged three secrets that have enabled them to maximize their teenager-parent relationship. These are not difficult, but they do require the parent to take the initiative and to be consistent in the pursuit of these activities.

Devote one-on-one time to your teenager. There is no substitute for spending both high quality and huge quantities of time with the teen. Their minds and bodies are raging with feelings and information they have never experienced before. They need to have their questions answered, but they can only ask those questions of someone they deeply trust and whom they sense has an unquestionable love for them.

Kids are the product of our devotion to them. Teenagers are in their last phase of development before leaving home. They need the attention and the advice that only parents can provide. Schedule dates with each teenager. Go places together, alone, and be a friend. It's your last chance to nurture them intensively. It may well be their last chance to absorb the values and perspectives they will need to make it in life.

Get to know their friends. Teenagers are very affected by how people respond to their friends. And their friends have a tremendous degree of influence on the attitudes and behaviors of your kids. Get to know who those influence agents are and befriend them as best you can. There are some very major limits on this, of course. You're not going to hang out at the movies or shop at the mall with them regularly. You may, however, find that the relationship you build with peer influencers can have a positive effect on both your child and his or her friends, if you are appropriately involved.

Discuss your actions. This is predominantly true in the case of disciplinary actions. Teenagers want to know "why" something is done, especially when it dramatically affects them. Their understanding of the motivations for our behavior is a great learning tool. Accommodate their desire to know why you have the rules, regulations, traditions and expectations that shape your responses to them. It can only help them to mature more intelligently and more confidently.

WORKING WITH KIDS WHO AREN'T YOURS

Youth workers have unique opportunities to influence teens. Those who work with kids who attend church activities have a special opportunity because many of the teens are there by choice and are searching for the kinds of answers Christianity can provide for them Much of what has just been said regarding the role of parents applies to youth workers as well. Create a positive learning environment in which they feel wanted, safe and respected; work on the basis of a well-honed and clearly developed philos ophy of teen development and ministry; and never forget that the deeper your relationship with a teenager, the greater your potential for positive influence.

Kids don't go to church for sermons, lectures and games. They attend because they want truth, they want help and they want to be accepted and loved. Churches or groups of people that provide kids with such nurturing qualities will gain ardent followers.

What kinds of specific tasks can a youth worker from a church engage in that will attract and retain the involvement of a teen? The research shows that it varies by age group, by region of the country and according to the religious background and spiritual training of the individual. Overall, the most helpful activities you might pursue are these:

Befriend the students. Let them know that they have an older person who understands and cares about them, and who will be there when needed.

Encourage them. Life is a series of victories and failures to teens—and most kids believe they lose more often than they win. Being a teenager is like growing up in a long tunnel; it never seems to end and there doesn't seem to be any light anywhere. You can provide the light through your encouragement.

Introduce them to serious Christianity. If kids come to a church, they do not need to be baby-sat. The chances are good that they are anxious to learn about spiritual truth. Don't neglect the privilege and opportunity you have to help them penetrate the spiritual darkness in their lives. Provide practical Bible lessons and useful biblical principles they can apply immediately in their lives. Build the spiritual foundation that will carry them through life. Never fear losing a teen because he or she is introduced to authentic Christianity; do so with sensitivity and then let God's Spirit handle the rest.

Help them with real-life problems. Sometimes you may be dragged into some of the seemingly petty issues in their lives: relational fallout, academic struggles, family misunderstandings, etc. Exploit the opening afforded to you to show them Christianity in action. Helping them with their real problems is a side of faith that often gets overlooked by churches and church leaders. However, assisting them with homework, helping them resolve conflicts, assisting them in their job hunt and similar activities are means of showing them that the family of Christ looks out for one another and integrates faith into all walks of our lives.

Provide them with lifestyle alternatives. Frankly, the world is constantly seducing teenagers with unbiblical alternatives. What can you offer as an option that would serve their needs, satisfy their desires and please God? Sometimes it's as simple as allowing kids to visit you for lunch (rather than to hang out with gangs) or to borrow a video you own (instead of journeying to the local cinema to watch less suitable fare). Teenagers weigh their alternatives. The better the options you can make available to them, the more likely they are to choose the more edifying or appropriate options.

Youth workers also have a great opportunity to help parents by keeping in communication with them about their kids. It is not the job of a youth worker to replace a parent or to instruct a parent on how to raise a child. However, providing the parent with honest feedback from a biblical perspective is often appreciated—and unique.

WATCHING TOMORROW TODAY

Teenagers can be a ball of contradictions, agonizingly honest or stubborn in their worldviews and appallingly immature in their decision making. But these are the leaders of the coming decades, the people who will dictate the quality of life that boomers, builders and seniors will experience in their "golden years." These young people represent perhaps our most significant legacy to the world. And for their development we will answer to God some day, having been allowed to be stewards of their development. The values, perspectives, beliefs and skills we help to implant in them today will largely determine the future of the world.

No pressure....

Notes

1. The proportion of marriages that end in divorce is currently 27 percent. This is substantially different from the 50 percent claimed by most media. The 50 percent notion is derived by dividing the number of divorces in a calendar year by the number of marriages in that same year. Obviously, these two numbers have nothing to do with each other, and thus create a meaningless statistic. We have found that of all the individuals who have been married, about one out of every four experiences a divorce. Incidentally, second (and subsequent) marriages experience an even higher divorce rate than do first marriages. For a more complete discussion, see chapter 4 in George Barna's *The Future of the American Family* (Chicago: Moody Press, 1993).

2. See the research alluded to in the following books: Judith Wallerstein and Sandra Blakeslee, *Second Chances* (New York: Ticknor & Fields, 1989); Arlene Skolnick and Jerome Skolnick, *Families in Transition* (Glenview, Ill.: Scott, Foresman & Co., sixth edition, 1989).

More Informative Resources from George Barna.

:h eting
/-Step Guide

leaders who want to
the ideas from
er books, here's a
ased guide. Put
marketing strategies
, discover and apply
ue vision for your
nd maximize your
ss in your community.

250p
7.14049

Evangelism that Works

A picture of the unsaved in the U.S. today and the methods that are reaching them. Provides leaders with practical real-life tools for the task.

Hardcover • 180p
ISBN 08307.17390

The Frog in the Kettle

If we share Christ's mission of reaching the world, we have to understand needs. This book gives a projection of the future and how we as Christians need to respond.

Trade • 235p
ISBN 08307.14278

User Friendly Churches

Discover the characteristics that today's healthiest churches hold in common and learn how to develop biblical, user-friendly strategies for reaching people.

Trade • 191p
ISBN 08307.14731

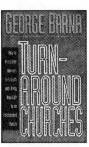

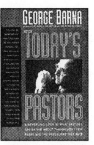

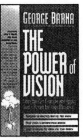

al America
a Report

the direction our
eading in terms of
liefs, lifestyles and
ts. This all-new
ides an insider's look
pidly changing
lso helps readers
those trends in the
Scripture and God's
e world.

• 300p
7.17153

Turnaround Churches

Discover how dozens of churches have made the transition from stagnation to growth—from the pastors who took part in turning the churches around. A view of the techniques many churches are using to rekindle the flame of growth and renewal.

Paperback • 204p
ISBN 08307.16572

Today's Pastors

In the tradition of his best-selling book, *The Frog in the Kettle*, George Barna takes his analysis of the church one step further—this time by taking the pulse of the person at the top. Examines the way ministers feel about themselves, the work they do, their colleagues and the congregations they serve.

Hardcover • 180p
ISBN 08307.15916

The Power of Vision

George Barna's message to thousands of church leaders who have said that they are struggling to capture God's vision for their ministries. It will help readers build a bridge between their own strategies and God's ideal plan for the future. Includes Bible studies on vision for church involvement.

Paperback • 300p
ISBN 08307.16017

Regal Books
A Division of Gospel Light